I0057142

WHAT'S INSIDE HERE

This book of clear, concise short-form explanations consists of two General Business sections with three more targeted categories underneath each General section. The General sections are broken out by their similarities in the various areas of business.

SECTION 1:   SECTION 2:
Finance   Marketing
Investing   Strategy
Accounting   Management

The goal here is to create understanding of important business terms, concepts, and ideas for New and Beginner business people who may not have a traditional or formalized business education or training.

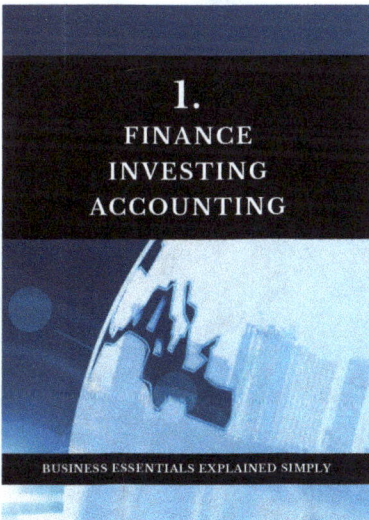

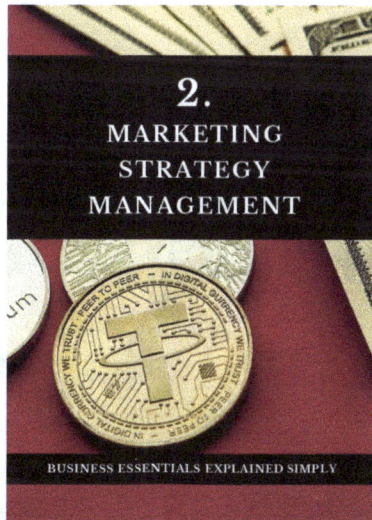

1.
FINANCE
INVESTING
ACCOUNTING

BUSINESS ESSENTIALS EXPLAINED SIMPLY

2.
MARKETING
STRATEGY
MANAGEMENT

BUSINESS ESSENTIALS EXPLAINED SIMPLY

Goldart Consulting LLC
(888) 203 - 6419
stuartg@goldartconsulting.com
www.goldartconsulting.com

© Goldart Publishing LLC. 2024
All rights reserved

FINANCE

BUSINESS BASICS EXPLAINED SIMPLY

1.

"BREAK-EVEN"

A Break-even is the point where a business or a product is not at a profit or a loss in its activities, but it's in a state of equilibrium as pertains to the balance of revenue and expenses. Many companies or products lose money early on in their activities, so the Break-even analysis calculates the point where that equilibrium of revenue and expense meets.

Generally to calculate a Break-even, we develop a gross margin figure—the amount of money we make on a unit of sales—as a dollar amount or percentage of revenue, then divide that in the total fixed expenses. The result will be the break-even point.

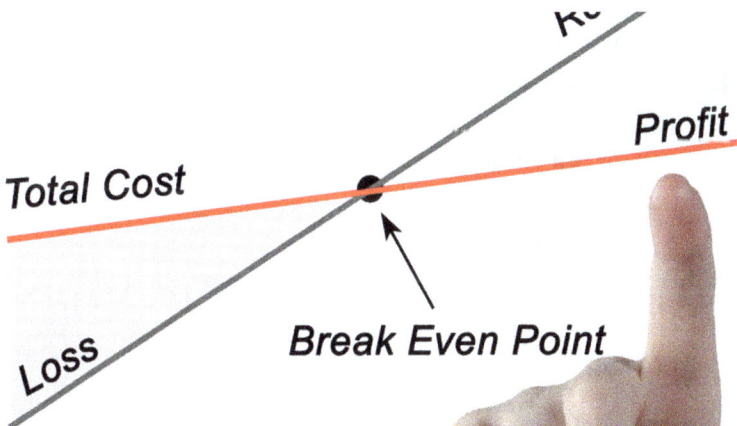

2.

"LIQUID / ILLIQUID"

In business, Liquid means how easy an asset can be turned into cash that can be used. Obviously, that means that cash is the most liquid of assets. But other assets can be made liquid relatively quickly, like public-traded stocks or a business's Accounts Receivable.

Illiquid assets are those that cannot be easily turned into cash for use. A Picasso painting for instance is a valuable asset, but not very liquid.

Liquidity is also a measurement of how liquid a person's or a business's assets are. One is said to be liquid when they have a sufficient level of liquid assets and the converse is true with illiquidity.

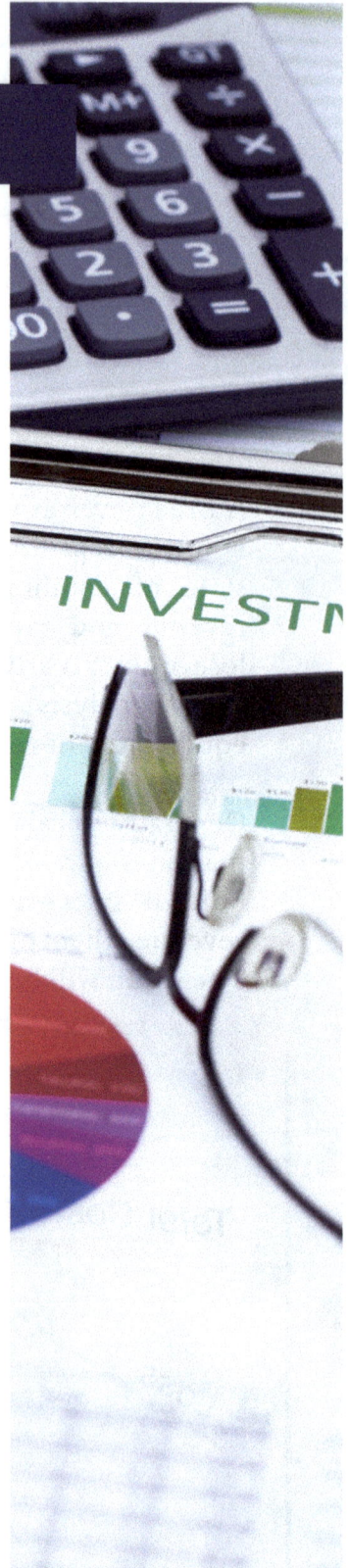

3.

"WORKING CAPITAL"

Working Capital is an accounting term that describes a net quantity of liquid assets the company has. It is calculated as the difference between Current Assets minus Current Liabilities.

Current Assets are those assets that are or can be turned into cash easily like Cash, Accounts Receivable and ready Inventory. Current Liabilities are those liabilities that must be paid in a short period of time, usually less than one year. The difference between these two Current calculations, which is Working Capital, generates a figure that speaks to a company's ability to pay its bills and other expenses in a soon-to-come period of time.

Generally, one wants their company to have higher, but not excessive, Working Capital.

4.

"TIME VALUE OF MONEY"

This is an important concept in the valuation of assets. Put simply, a dollar received today is worth more than a dollar received a year from now. Because if I receive a dollar today, I can invest it and receive interest on it for a year. Therefore, in a year I will have my dollar plus some interest more. This is the Time Value of Money.

In business, even more options exist. A dollar received today can be invested in high-returning projects or could pay off high-rate credit card debts.

So when discussing terms with both vendors and customers, remember the maxim that a dollar today is worth more than a dollar tomorrow and use it to make decisions accordingly.

5.

"PRINCIPAL AND INTEREST"

Principal and Interest are two financial elements of a loan agreement. Principal is the total amount of money that is borrowed in the loan and Interest is the rate of payment made for the pleasure of having that loan.

As an example, we can have a loan for $10,000 with an interest of 10%. Here the Principal amount is the $10,000 and that is the total amount that needs to be repaid. Additionally, most loans come with an Interest payment requirement, which means the borrower must pay a fee based on a rate times the total principle amount. In our scenario, 10% of $10,000 or doing the math, $1,000.

So in this scenario the total payments of Principal and Interest from borrower to lender is $11,000.

6.

"SECURED/UNSECURED DEBT"

The debt a company has, ie., monies owed to either a person, business or institution, can be Secured or Unsecured. The difference between these two is whether some asset of the company has been pledged specifically against the money owed. This becomes very important if a company were to go bankrupt.

An example: A company has borrowed $20,000 from a bank and pledged a building purchased with the money against that loan. Now that loan (read: debt) is secured by the value of the building. If the company were to go bankrupt, the bank would have the right to sell the building to recoup the money on its loan.

Unsecured debt is not tied to any specific asset, and is much riskier as a result. The lender can only recoup money if there are leftover assets in the business.

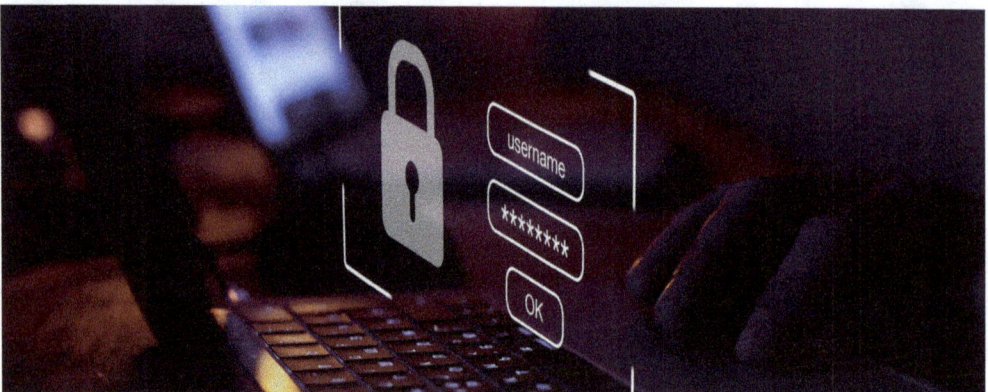

7.

"ALTERNATIVE LENDING"

While this term always sounds a little bit like loan sharking related to the mafia, Alternative Lending is a legitimate and often necessary lending avenue for many small businesses struggling with their business's cash flow needs. The term Alternative Lending encompasses many different lending vehicles that traditional Banks and other mainstream lending institutions do not offer, including workday loans, loans at high interest rates, loans against specific revenue payments and other even more creative vehicles.

It is specifically that traditional banks don't make these type of loans that the name alternative comes into play. These funding sources are not recommended for the long-term as their rates are prohibitive. But when necessary...do what you must do.

8.

"PRESENT VALUE"

When Finance people consider investments and the price they are willing to pay for some asset, they usually are evaluating the cashflows that the asset will bring over time. The concept of the Time Value of Money tells us that future cashflows are worth less than the cash received today.

So often potential investors or purchasers of assets will analyze the future cashflows in their Present Value. This is calculated by "discounting" future cash flows into their value today, or Present Value. The calculation is a bit complex and depends on the rate of discounting and the time over which the discount occurs but the concept is important in evaluating investments. So remember, $1,000 received five years from now is worth less in today's dollars.

10

9.

"FUTURE VALUE

Similar to Present Value, yet in some senses its opposite, Future Value utilizes the concept of the Time Value of Money to interpret the value in the future of some asset. The Future Value is largely based on the cash flows the asset generates over time based on an estimate of its compounded growth rates.

Again similar to a present value analysis, the calculation of a Future Value is complex. It takes into account a prevailing interest rate, usually a company's cost of capital, the time in the future being evaluated for, and the cash flows expected. It is a corollary to the CAGR (discussed herein), but looks at final value number and not a growth rate percentage.

Many business valuations are often driven by Future Value estimations.

10.

"MULTIPLE-OF-EARNINGS VALUATION METHOD"

Essentially, there are three main ways that companies are valued when someone or some company is considering making an investment or purchasing outright an existing company. The easiest and most common is known as the Multiple of Earning Method.

Simply, it is a matter of taking some metric of the earnings of a company and multiplying that by a some figure called a multiple. The multiple is most often a number that is standard within an industry. So if the average bank company is valued at eight times its earnings, one takes the earnings of some bank to be valued and multiply it times eight. Note: The metric of earnings may vary between industries and companies (Net Income, EBITDA, Net Revenue, Free Cashflow, etc.)

11.

"DISCOUNTED CASHFLOW (DCF) VALUATION METHOD"

The second most common way of evaluating a company for investment or outright buying is the Discounted Cashflow Method. It is much more difficult and complex than the Multiple of Earnings method.

In essence, an analysis is done that forecasts the cashflows that will come from a company over a period of time, often ten years. Then these cashflows are "discounted" into their Present Value using an appropriate discount rate, which is often a prevailing interest rate or the cost of capital of a potential acquirer.

It can be difficult to accurately forecast the cashflows of a company, so this method has risks.

12.

"SUM-OF-THE-PARTS VALUATION"

The third main Valuation method of companies is known as the Sum-of-the-Parts method. This is generally used for large corporations that have various business lines and legal entities under the one conglomerated company.

Essentially, giant companies are oftentimes really just several smaller companies under one umbrella. So to value the larger company, it is often advisable to try to evaluate each of the smaller parts and add up the values. This gives a sense of the value of the larger company as whole if was broken up into its constituent pieces. Hence, the name. Obviously this only works for large companies with many different divisions.

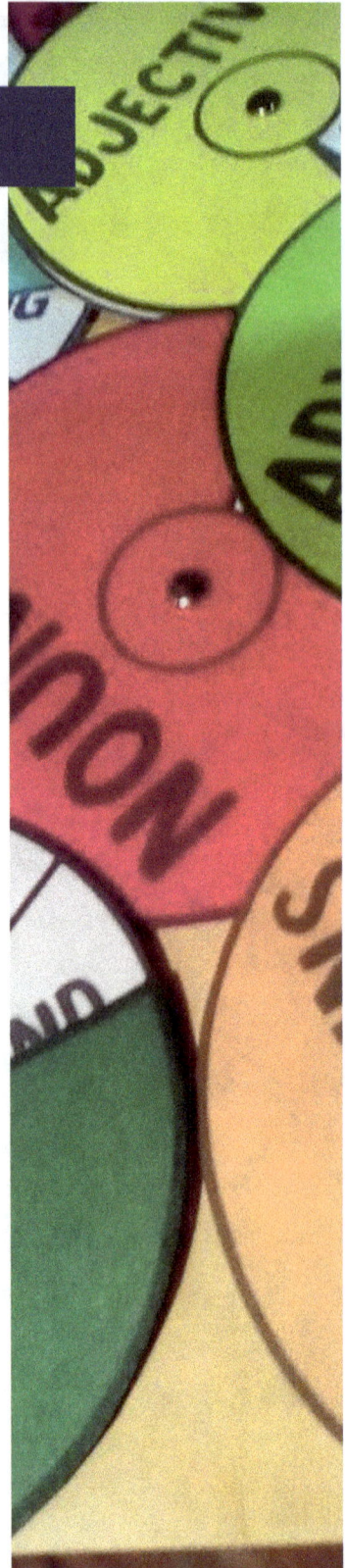

13.

"OPPORTUNITY COST"

In Business we have limitations on certain assets such as Cash and Time. As such we need to make decisions on where to invest these most precious of assets. Since generally we cannot bet on all things at once, that means that certain opportunities will be pursued while others will not. From this state of affairs comes the idea of an Opportunity Cost.

Opportunity Cost is the price we pay for pursuing one activity while not pursing another. In theory, doing one activity precludes us from doing something else with our limited assets. So in business, we think of an opportunity lost and recognize that we want the activity we chose to create a greater return than the one we chose not to attempt.

14.

"RETURN ON INVESTMENT (ROI)"

Businesses make investments with the hope of getting a return that is more money than we originally invested all factors considered. We call the extra money earned the Return on the Investment.

In Business we calculate this amount in a different manner than we do in regular life. In Business we recognize that we have many opportunities to invest in and so there is an Opportunity Cost for making one investment over another. So when we make an investment, we take into account the cost of choosing this option so that for a return to be a good investment, it must return our money plus a rate greater than our Opportunity Cost.

15.

"SUNK COSTS"

Mistakes get made in business, especially with Investments and spending. And oftentimes, a bad spending or investment decision occurs, and with that, money invested is not retrieved, or a return on the investment is not possible. Those monies are said to be Sunk Costs. Essentially with the investment or spending that was made, an understanding that the monies are not recoverable is attained.

This concept is used to understand that even though the money was spent and lost, one should NOT figure those monies into the future decisions that need to made. Just because I spent $1,000 on a machine that doesn't work, it doesn't mean I should consider that investment in the next decision I make on buying another machine that does. The first investment is sunk and not relevant to future investment decisions.

16.

"FINANCIAL RATIOS"

These are a series of calculations that are designed to give an analyzer a sense of the status of a company. When the numbers are good, these ratios speak to the health and stability of the company. Conversely, when the numbers are poor, they speak to instability and lack of financial health.

Common financial ratios include but are not limited to Coverage and Debt Ratios, which speak to the company's ability to manage its debt, and Efficiency Ratios which speak to a company's ability to effectively utilize its assets.

All together, Financial Ratios can be an important tool to track health and progress over time.

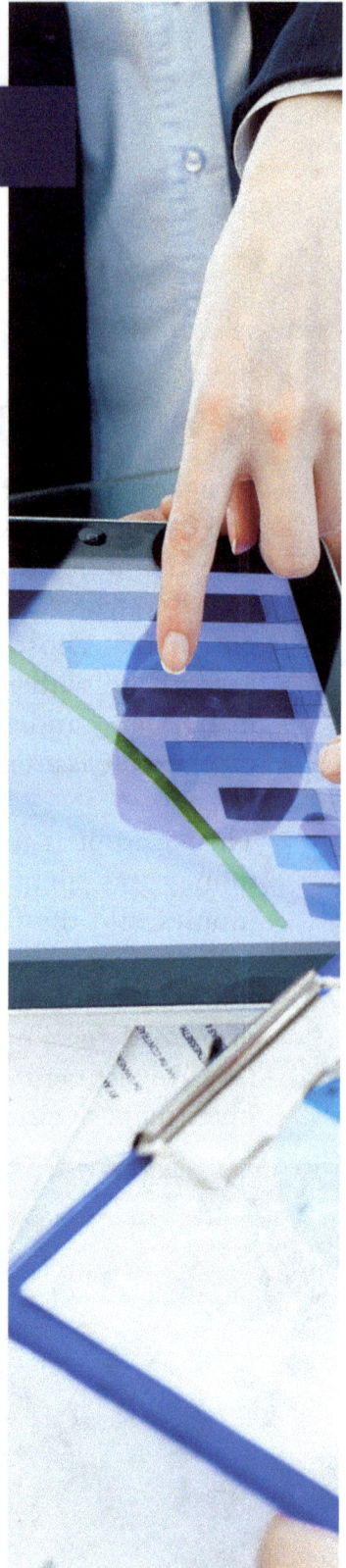

17.

"COVERAGE RATIOS"

A type of Financial Ratio, Coverage Ratios focus completely and specifically on a company's ability to handle its debt and debt service. In other words, if the company can make its Principal and Interest payments on a timely basis and with sufficient cash to continue to fund the operations of the business.

Generally, but not always, the calculation is a function of projected cash flow divided into some form of debt servicing payments. If cash flow is a high multiple of debt servicing payments, it means the company has plenty of ability to fulfill its commitments. If the the multiple is small or even worse, fractional, it means the company is in financial jeopardy.

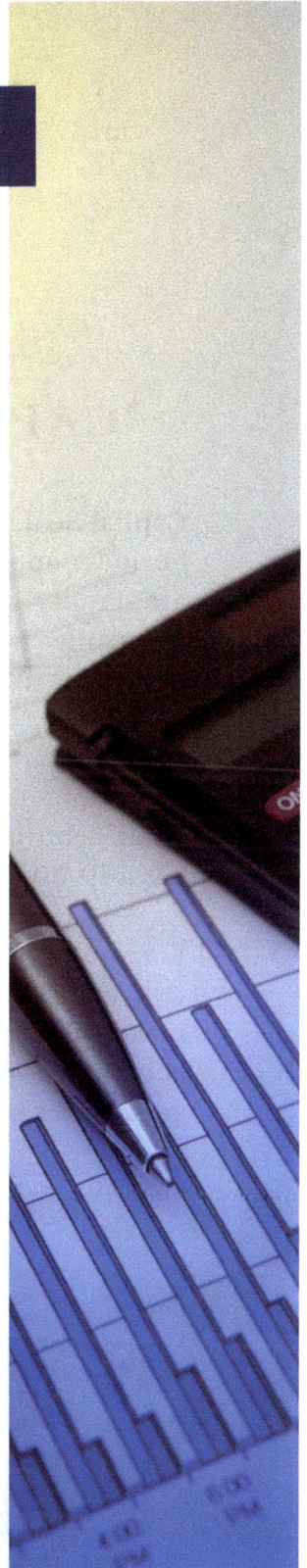

18.

"CAPITAL STRUCTURE"

Capital Structure refers to how a company finances its business operations. The two elements that are used are Equity and Debt (previously defined). Most companies will use a combination of both elements to most effectively and efficiently finance the business.

If 70% of the capital a company uses to fund its operations comes from Equity sales and 30% comes from debt (loans, bonds) it is said that this company has a 70-30 Capital Structure.

For most companies, having more debt increases the risk associated with the company because it must make its Principal and Interest payments. But, companies with no debt are not taking enough risk to get a better return.

19.

"PAYMENT TERMS"

Payment Terms is when a vender offers you a discount on the total cost of your invoice when you pay your bill in a certain defined time frame. Generally, but not always, it is an incentive or a reward to a customer to pay the invoice and bills early or even in advance.

They come in various different shapes and sizes, but a very common example is known as 2/10 net 30. In this example, the purchaser is rewarding you paying off a bill quickly by giving you a 2% discount to pay the invoice in 10 days.

This is one example. Nothing is a hard, fast rule or law as payment terms can take many different forms and are usually negotiated between two parties to a deal.

Terms and Condi

using this service you are deemed to ha
rms and conditions for contributers:

1 – 6: General Terms and Conditions
Limitation of liability

content of our websites has been compiled with
wever, we cannot assume any liability for the up-t
of the pages.

rivacy policy

will save your order and
r details. Your data will   within the

rms of payment

he payment shall be
ght to supply only ag

nvoice amount is to
e amount is to be
tes has been co
ne any liability f

ayment shall be
supply only a

ranty and lia

rranty and li

tation of

tent of o
r, we ca
he page

of payment

payment shall be made either via
to supply only against payment in advance.

ce amount is to be transferred within 10 days to our
mount is to be transferred to us within 10 days of the
has been compiled with care and to the best of ou
any liability for the up-to-dateness, completeness o

hange these terms at any time.

I acknowledge that I have read and agree to the a
Conditions

Please sign here _____

Read caref

20.

"BURN RATE"

As I always say, cash is more important than your mother. When we are out of cash, and out of external credit lines to draw on cash, we are essentially out of business. So we track cash as we would track our blood and oxygen.

Burn Rate is the rate at which a company is losing Net Cash on a monthly basis. If you are net losing $5,000 in cash every month, and your cash balance is only $30,000, then you only have six months of cash on hand before a catastrophe occurs. So calculate your Burn Rate based on the past six months of net cash production or deficit. It is a countdown clock that cannot be ignored, and must be managed to protect your future.

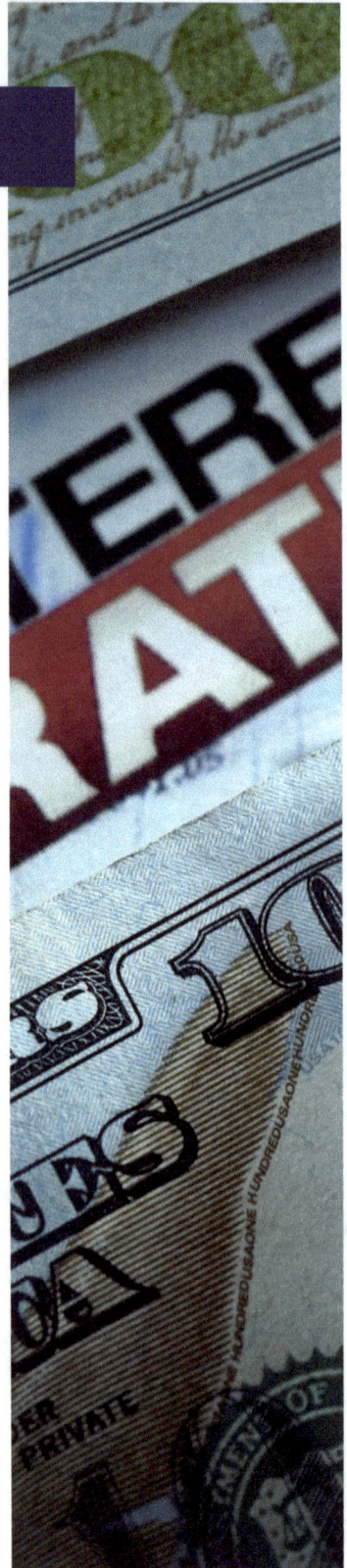

21.

"COMPOUNDED ANNUAL GROWTH RATE (CAGR)"

In Business, the rate of growth of earnings of a company is a very important metric that speaks to its financial health and future prospects. Investors take growth rates very seriously when considering whether or not to make an investment or buy stock, as companies with higher growth rates generally produce greater returns to investors over time.

The Compounded Annual Growth Rate metric, known as CAGR in the financial industry, is a calculation that shows the growth rate of an item, usually earnings, but occasionally revenue or cash flow. It calculates the rate of growth taking into account compounding, which means the annual growth rate year over year. The calculation is quite difficult, but the concept is essential to understand.

22.

Return on Invest

Period Comparison

Item	Cost Per Item
1	$4.00
2	$5.00
3	$13.00
4	$11.50
	$10.00
6	$13.27
7	$14.51
8	$15.75
9	$17.00
10	$18.24
	$18.24
12	$20.72
13	
14	$22.56
15	$25.34
16	$26.72
Total	

"RISK - RETURN TRADEOFF"

It is a core understanding in investments, and in life, that in order to take greater risk on something, there is an expectation of a greater return in reward for taking the risk. This is known as the Risk-Return Trade-off.

What is a sufficient return vis-à-vis a risk is independent and relative for each person and company. There are many factors that play into it, but in general in Business, we should never take on greater risk if we are not going to be rewarded for it in terms of either some quantitative or a qualitative measurement.

Taking on risk without a commensurate return is a bad decision.

24

23.

"CAPITAL RAISE"

In the life cycle of a business, there often comes a time when a business will need additional monies beyond what the company is generating to help fund its growth or make necessary payments. At this point, most companies will try to raise money from investors, and this process is known as a Capital Raise.

In this sense, a company will try to sell shares in its company—shares being ownership in the company—in return for the needed funds. A Capital Raise is completed when the funds are received by the company and the transfer of shares has been made to the Investor delivering the funds.

Capital Raises are an essential part of growing, as most companies cannot fund their growth solely by their operations alone.

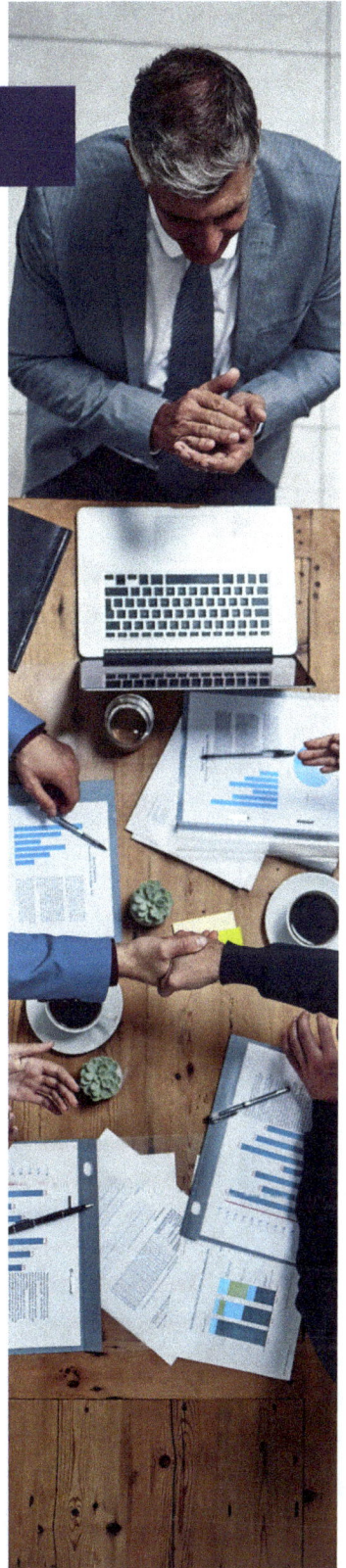

24.

"COST OF CAPITAL / THE HURDLE RATE"

The Cost of Capital, which works as the Hurdle Rate for most situations, is a calculation of overall financing rates for a company based on its capital structure. It is based on both the Cost of Debt and the Cost of Equity in its calculations.

The Hurdle Rate is a basic rate that any investment must achieve in order for a company to give the go-ahead to undertake the project. Most companies will use their Cost of Capital as the base Hurdle Rate.

In essence, it means that a project or investment must generate a rate of return greater than the Hurdle Rate, thus the name. Say the Hurdle Rate is 10%, a project's projections must show a return on investment greater than this percentage to be considered for approval.

25.

"COMPOUNDING"

Compounding in business is the mathematical result that occurs when something happens repeatedly over many periods of time. If something happens again and again over many years, the end result will have exponentially grown as a function of the continued string of events.

An example: We have $1,000 and we earn 10% each year. The first year, we received $100 in interest. When we add this to our initial money, we have $1,100. When we receive interest in the 2nd year, it will be $110, giving us a total of $1,210. In the 3rd year, we receive interest of $121 giving us $1,331.

This increasing interest effect, from $100 to $121 over two years is Compounding.

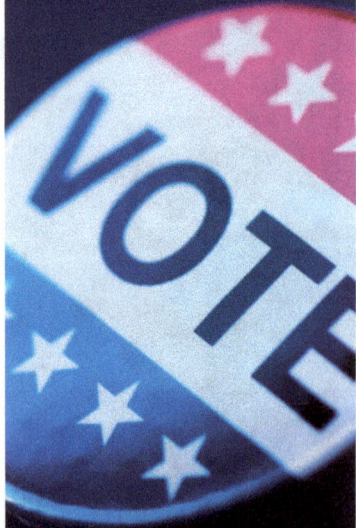

26.

"VOTING INTEREST / VOTING CONTROL"

With shares in a company, also known as stock or equity, it is generally arranged that one share equals one vote. So when one owns a share, one has a Voting Interest in the company.

However, it is possible to setup different classes of stock, and give one class of stock the power to have greater number of votes per share. Some companies have done either 10 or 20 votes per share with a certain class of shares.

When you have over 50% of the voting shares in a company, it is said that you have Voting Control. That is, on any corporate vote, you control the majority so in theory, the vote will go as you decide it given your majority stake.

27.

"ECONOMIC INTEREST / ECONOMIC CONTROL"

One has an Economic Interest in a company when one owns shares in a company. So if that company earns money or pays dividends, as the owners of shares, you will receive your percentage of the cashflows that the company distributes to its shareholders.

An example: I own 10% of a company, so my economic interest in the company is 10%. If the company earns $1 Million in a given year and plans to distribute those profits to its shares, my 10% economic interest will allow me to receive $100,000 as a result.

Economic Control is when a person owns more than a 50% of an Economic Interest in a company.

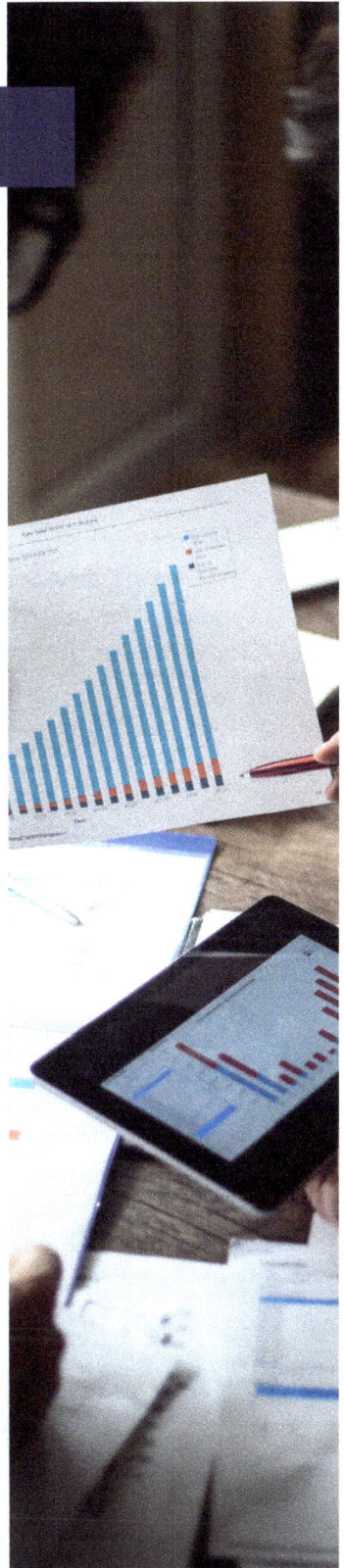

28.

"BOTTOMS-UP ANALYSIS"

Generally there are two different types of business analyses in terms of financial matters. Bottoms-Up Analysis is where the analysis is built from the most basic level of elements, then driven upwards following the logic the business necessitates.

An example: A sneaker company needs to develop a forecast of its revenue. The Bottoms-Up Analysis builds the analysis by asking the question: "What is the average price of the sneaker?" Then it asks how many sneakers is it estimated will be sold in a given period. These two are multiplied together to get the total revenue forecasted to be made for those sneakers in a given period.

Bottoms-Up Analysis forces the analyst to understand more deeply the individual elements of an analysis.

29.

"TOP-DOWN ANALYSIS"

The second type of financial analysis is called Top Down Analysis because the analyst choses a top figure first without analyzing the underlining elements that drive that figure.

An Example: In Top-Down Analysis, if a sneaker company was asked to forecast its revenue for the coming year, it can merely choose the number $1 Million as the revenue of the year. The figure could be based on previous year's figures and an understanding overall of the elements that are projected to effect a total revenue number.

Top-Down Analysis is easier, but inferior to Bottoms-up analysis but it is both easier and faster to do which is the reason many Small Businesses use it.

30.

"INVESTOR DECK"

When one is looking to raise capital for their business, one needs a communication document that shares the planning. In Business we call that document an Investor Deck. Oftentimes the Investor Deck is a printed PDF Powerpoint presentation and acts merely as a summary of a completed business plan.

Typically, an Investor Deck includes several slides that communicate to the reader important information including an analysis of the financial projections, the overall market environment for the company or product, a thorough analysis of competition, the requests for funding, etc.

An Investor Deck's importance cannot be underestimated as investors will rely on it.

31.

"PAYBACK PERIOD"

Payback Period is a calculation that businesses do to understand how long it will take to get a return on an investment. There are various different versions of a Payback Period analysis and some are very complicated, taking into account cost of capital and other factors in an investment.

However, the simplest version of the calculation is as follows: If a project costs $10,000 and generates a return of $2,000 per year, by dividing one into the other we can see that the simple payback period is five years. This is how long will it take to get our money back.

In general, businesses should complete this calculation on a forecasted basis before the project starts and look to achieve the shortest Payback Period possible on their investments, all other things being equal.

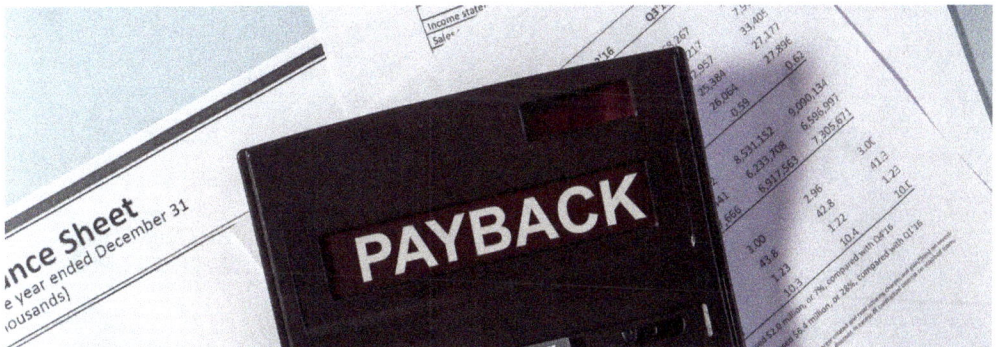

32.

"NET LOSS CARRY FORWARD"

Small Businesses have losses often. It is a sad fact of Business world. There is one good thing associated with that and it comes from the tax code. When you have an annual loss in your business, this loss can be "carried forward" to reduce taxable income in future years.

Example: If your business loses $5,000 in a given year, you are able to apply that loss against a profit of some number the next year so that no or reduced taxes will be paid in that future year. The gross profit is reduced by the $5,000 previous year loss.

In fact, in many cases, you can apply the loss against a gain in past years, and ask for a refund if all the guidelines are met.

33.

"ARBITRAGE"

Arbitrage is the concept of taking advantage of price distortions in a marketplace. While these distortions do not come very often, and are even less often capable of being exploited, from time to time they do exist and can lead to substantial profits.

An example: Imagine gold is selling in one country for $1,000 an ounce, and is selling in another country for $1,500 an ounce. It would be smart business to buy gold at $1,000 in one country and immediately sell it at $1,500 in the other. This price distortion creates an Arbitrage opportunity. In theory enough people would do this Arbitrage until the price in one country matches the other country, and the opportunity disappears. Arbitrage is very hard to do with physical assets, but is more common with non-physical financial assets.

34.

"DEBT SERVICE"

Debt Service, or servicing the debt, is when a business returns principal and pays interest to people or institutions like banks who have lent them money. Those payments together, which are usually periodic and outlined in a loan agreement, are called Debt Service.

Servicing the debt is important, for if a company does not make the Debt Service payments that are outlined in the lending agreement, the company can be forced into bankruptcy by its lenders because of the non-payment. So it is essential that a company manages its cashflow in such a manner that it can service its outstanding debt, meaning it can make regular principal and interest payments to its lenders, and thereby avoid bankruptcy.

35.

"LEVERED / LEVERAGE"

In Business, Leverage is the state of having debt in the business, and also it's a measurement of how much debt exists in a business's capital structure. It is called this because having debt allows shareholders to expand the power of the shares they have in the company by borrowing money, and not selling away shares in the company (only 100% can exist).

With Leverage, and even increasing Leverage, a company becomes more risky because ultimately the company needs to pay back both the principal and the interest that the company has borrowed. Thus companies must watch and track carefully their Leverage ratios (calculations that measure company risk due to the amount of debt they have) and be sure to manage their cashflow appropriately to ensure Leverage does not put the company at risk of failure.

36.

"DILUTION"

Dilution is an important term in business as it concerns equity ownership in a company after a portion of the company has been sold. Much as adding water to some mixture will dilute the mixture, a similar principle occurs with Dilution and stock ownership. Its importance pertaining to control of the company cannot be overestimated.

When an existing company sells a portion of its shares to a 3rd party, the current shareholders stake in the company is diluted. Example: If two people own 50% of a company and they sell 30% to an outside party, the percentages of the shareholders is diluted. How this Dilution occurs can affect how the company is managed and run. If they give up shares equally, both will only have 35% in the company, thus no control of the company. If only one person gives up shares the other person has control.

37.

"IMPUTED VALUE"

Imputed Value is a way of discerning the value of a whole company based on the sale of a portion of the company. It is a very important metric in fundraising.

If, for example, 10% of a company is sold to an investor for $50,000 (the Imputed Value) the value implied as a function of this transaction is $500,000. Likewise, if 33% of the company is sold for $1 million, the company is being valued at $3 million.

Oftentimes in fundraising, it is important to have an increasing valuation based on the imputed values of one's fundraising transactions, as it shows a company becoming more valuable in the marketplace.

38.

"CARRYING COSTS"

Carrying Costs are the related costs that come along with having Inventory over a period of time. While not a direct Inventory cost like raw materials, packaging supplies and finished products, these costs are incurred generally when one has and keeps inventory.

Classic examples include interest expense, storage /warehouse expense, insurance on products expense, etc.

To understand the true cost of holding inventory one must include the Carrying Costs with the cost of the direct inventory expenses ie., storage interest insurance, etc.

39.

"FACTORING"

Factoring is a form of financing a business through the selling of your Accounts Receivables. It is often a very expensive mode of financing as the cost can be as much as 15% or more of your sales. But it is a viable option for the desperate.

In essence, a company with Accounts Receivable will sell these rights to payment to a 3rd party lender, who will pay generally anywhere from 85-95% of the total value of the Accounts Receivable. So if the receivable is $10,000, the "factor" will factor the receivable and buy it, for example, for $9,000. The company receives the money, and the factor ultimately received the payment on the sale.

40.

"LOAN AGREEMENT"

An essential part of the loan process is signing a Loan Agreement, which explains the specific terms between the borrower and the lender. A Loan Agreement should always be written and signed regardless of the type of loan and regardless of who the loan is between.

A Loan Agreement should specify the principal amount, the interest rate, the repayment schedule of the loan, late fee penalties, and any other specific terms that may affect the loan, including default provisions if the borrower cannot repay the loan. It is essential to have a loaning agreement in place before exchanging money.

41.

"PRIVATE PLACEMENT MEMORANDUM (PPM)"

A PPM, (Private Placement Memorandum) is a securities document that a company shares with potential investors that will outline the terms, conditions, requirements, and other essential company operating information about the company as pertains to a private sale of shares in that company. It is a private document only shared with certain potential investors as the offering is not available to the general public, but only certain specific investors which the company chooses.

Important elements will be included like management team, corporate strategy, and marketing goals and tactics. Given the highly sensitive nature of this information, companies are rightly sensitive about the distribution of the information.

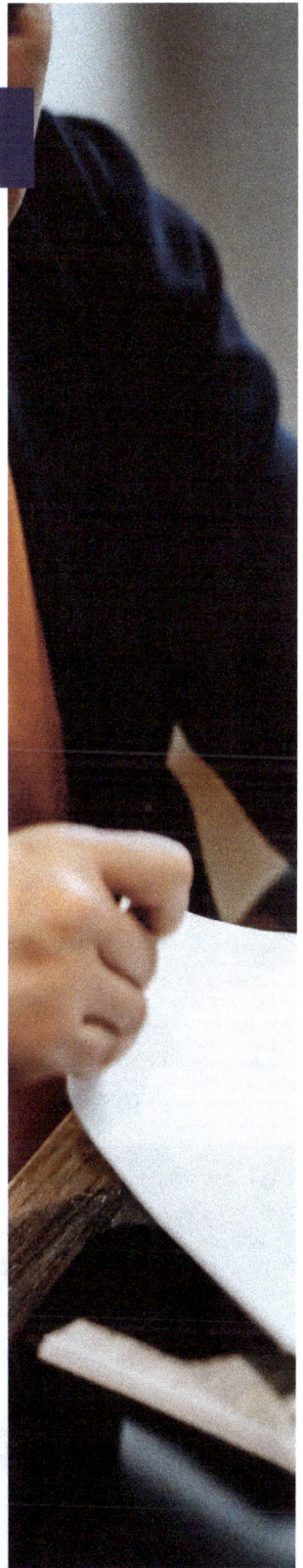

42.

"CAPITALIZATION RATE (CAP RATE)"

Essential to any income-generating Real Estate investment consideration is the calculation of the Capitalization Rate, often shortened in the industry to just Cap Rate. It is the financial calculation derived by taking the market value of the asset divided by the income the asset is expected to generate. This percentage derives the expected return from the financial investment in the asset.

Savvy Real Estate investors will often use the Cap Rate analysis as a means of comparing multiple different Real Estate investment opportunities to derive, which may be a better investment. As one can imagine, the higher percentage generated represents a better opportunity.

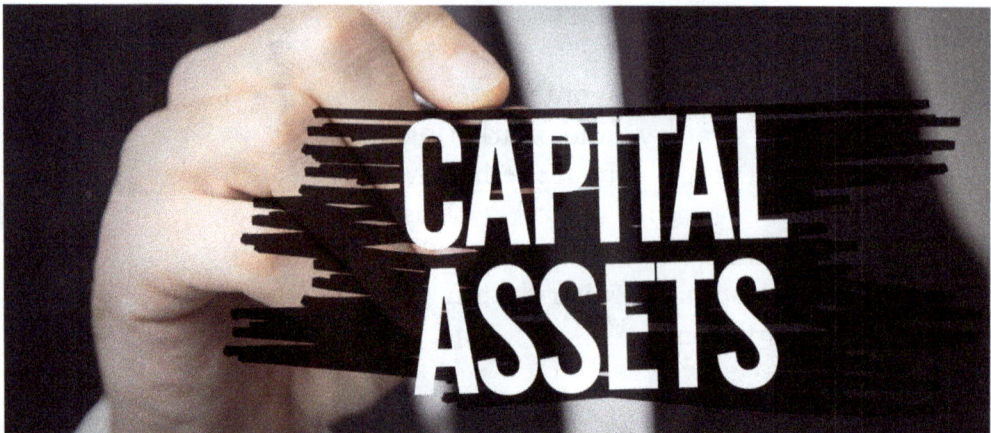

43.

"EBITDA"

This acronym stands plainly for Earning Before Interest, Taxes, Depreciation and Amortization. Most investors look at this version of profitability as a true sign of how the operations of a business are doing, excluding those elements that don't speak directly to the day-to-day running of the core fundamental business.

The things listed in the acronym are outside the core operations of the business. While they are still quite essential to the success of the business, they do not speak to the core of having a product and services that is trying to reach a market. So as a more basic look on progress or success, many investors will focus on this figure because if this number is not positive it truly speaks to problems in the core situation.

44.

"RECURRING REVENUE"

In some ways the dream of all small businesses and even large ones too, Recurring Revenue are those revenue streams that occur monthly without much effort, input, or marketing.

Some classic examples are monthly fees like bank account fees and the monthly base charges on your cable or telephone bill. These expenses reoccur each month, oftentimes due to a contract signed by a customer, and they reoccur again and again until the customers stop that arrangement.

Large sums of monthly Recurring Revenue are often a path to great financial success and investor interest. One should always be looking to develop them.

45.

"BLUE SKY LAWS"

Blue Sky Laws are state laws intended to protect investors from fraud, specifically fraudulent claims made by those people and companies looking to raise capital from investors. Since they are State laws, they will vary by each state, though similarities exist among the different state Blue Sky Laws.

In essence, Blue Sky Laws require sellers of shares known as issuers to register their securities for sale and provide investors with various and sufficient information that the potential investor can use to better understand all of the risks and opportunities associated with a potential investment. They are intended to limit extreme claims (promising the Blue Sky) made by the issuer as pertains to the offering and create liabilities for the issuers if fraud is deemed to have occurred as pertains to fraudulent claims made.

46.

"FORWARD-LOOKING / SAFE HARBOR STATEMENTS"

Forward-Looking Statements, also known as Safe Harbor Statements, are those statements made by companies that cannot be proven by a past fact, and are in fact statements about the future which the company is making but cannot be assumed or counted on to occur. Typical Forward-Looking Statements in business documents are all sorts of business forecasts such as revenue projections, profit and earnings forecast, market share assumptions, etc.

Companies in their securities filings and offering memorandum must mention that Forward Looking Statements are being made in the document so as to inform the reader (potential investor) that relying on these statements as facts is not correct, and risky given their nature as predictions or forecasts.

47.

"AN EXIT / EXIT STRATEGY"

In finance, an Exit is when the investors in a business sell their shares (stock) in a company they have invested in. They are essentially exiting the company, no longer being involved with it, by selling their stock to some other party. Exits are often seen as ways for initial investors in a company to be rewarded for the value in the company they have created.

Oftentimes business plans will speak of an Exit Strategy, which is the plan the current shareholders have for exiting the company. The two most common Exit Strategies are going public, selling shares to the public through a stock exchange like the Nasdaq or New York Stock Exchange, or being bought out–purchased by another company.

48.

"VENTURE CAPITAL"

In the areas of finance and raising capital, there are several terms used to describe various types of investors, and Venture Capital is often used as a catch-all to describe the type of investors. Also known by its initials, VC, Venture Capital is money invested in companies that are not publicly traded on a stock exchange, but are privately owned.

By definition, it is capital risked in a venture with the understanding that the investment can be lost entirely, but the investment is made with the hope of great financial returns in the future. It is this unique risk-reward trade-off in private companies that defines Venture Capital, as opposed to investment in public companies traded on a stock exchange, through the purchasing of stock, where the risk is less generally, but not always.

49.

"PRIVATE EQUITY"

Another term to describe a type of capital for investment, Private Equity is, in theory, capital that is used to take private those existing publicly-traded companies underperforming expectations. The investors are private, meaning they are not companies publicly traded on a stock exchange.

Private Equity investments are often made in companies that are not performing well for whatever reasons, and the Private Equity investor looks to take the company private, fix the problems at the company, often with the hope of relisting (relaunching) the company on a stock exchange in the future. Private Equity investors are normally very large private investment funds with billions of investable dollars under management. This financial size affords them the capacity to take over companies, large and small.

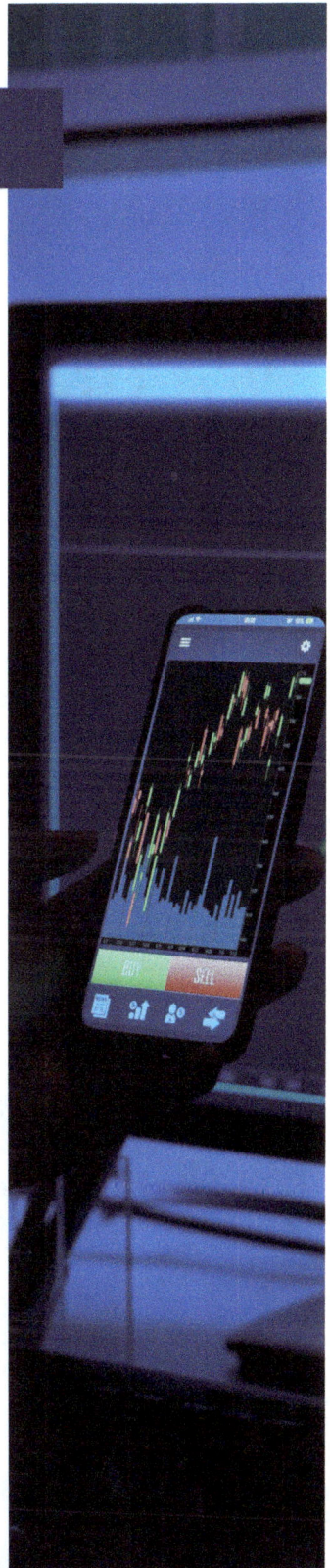

50.

"WHITE KNIGHT"

Often the hero of many Small Business dreams, the White Knight is normally an individual investor or a club of small investors, who make small but meaningful investments in start-up companies. They are called White Knights because usually they invest in companies that often otherwise don't receive investments because of the nature of the business or where the business is in its life cycle (too early or too small to attract other Venture Capital).

White Knight investors are often typically the second investor in a Small Business that's growing after the founders, who will have put in the start-up capital, be it cash or sweat equity (their personal efforts).

51.

"HEDGE FUND"

A Hedge Fund is a pooled investment instrument that has the ability to invest for the owners of the pool in countless investing strategies, from both long and short positions (see definitions) and even more exotic approaches. The investment pool is often limited by the by-laws of the fund, which govern what can and cannot be invested in.

The name comes from its original use, which allowed the investment managers to hedge trading positions to lower overall risk through their approach. However, the name has become a broader umbrella to mean all types of pooled investment vehicles. Often, but not always, access to Hedge Fund investment opportunities are limited to those investors with a proven level of investing experience and net worth.

52.

"PRE/POST MONEY VALUATION"

Pre-Money Valuation is the value of the equity in a business BEFORE the company has received a round of investment capital. Sometimes it's just an idea, othertimes it's an operating business, and others still it's just an amalgam of business assets like Intellectual property. But whichever state it's in, a company can have a value before it raises its first capital or additional capital. That value is its Pre-Money Valuation.

Obviously after a company has raised capital, its value has increased by virtue of its raising capital. Thus its Post-Money Valuation is an evaluation that captures its new funded valuation, which increases at least as much as the capital raised.

53.

"SERIES A, B, C ETC. ROUNDS"

Rounds of funding in finance are given names corresponding to the alphabet, with each succeeding round moving through and upwards. The Series Rounds usually follow after the other early rounds, such as Seed / Family and Friends and Angel investment, as they tend to be more formalized with advanced legal agreements, with larger sizes investments, and with more experienced institutions.

The Series Rounds are generally focused on growing companies, and depending on which letter round it is in its progression, those that have usually achieved a proof of concept, market launch, even some level of sales and establishment in their marketplace, though very early in their life cycle, and ultimate potential growth and development.

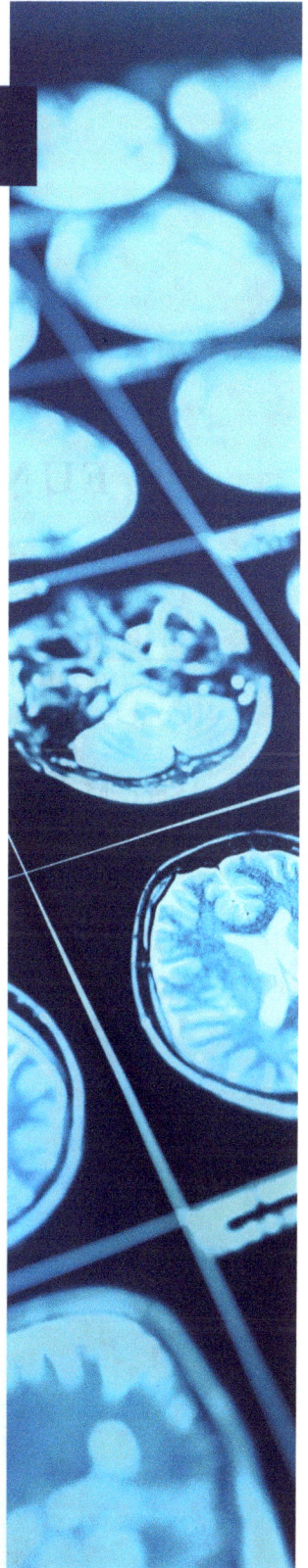

54.

"SEED MONEY / FUNDING / CAPITAL"

Seed Money (as known as Seed Funding and Seed Capital) is beginning funding to help develop an idea in its infancy. It is the 'seed' that hopes to grow into a fledging project or business in the future. And then of course, the hope is the sky.

Seed Money is generally provided by people close to the founders, often friends and family, with the goal of developing an idea, project or business in exchange for some level of equity participation (ownership) in the future business. Seed Money is a very risky investment as highly often the idea does not develop into a full fledged, profitable business.

55.

"FAMILY AND FRIENDS ROUND"

The first funding for most Small Businesses come from the Family and Friends Round, which is the seed money invested by the family and friends of the business founders. This money, along with monies invested in the business by the founders themselves, is the most common and most basic of funding source for the vast majority of Small Businesses.

These are generally very risky investments for the Family and Friends as too often the small business started will not be profitable in the long-term and the investment often ends up being worthless over time.

56.

"A DOWN ROUND"

In a perfect world, each round of financing is done at a higher valuation of the company. For example, the first round is done with a one million dollar valuation, and the next round is done at say, a five million dollar valuation. The progression in valuation is desired.

However, often a Down Round occurs, which is where a company raises capital at a lower valuation than a previous capital raise. This is a disappointment to be sure, and generally occurs because something has not gone right with the business plan or the investment market. However, when the company desperately needs a cash investment, it will do a Down Round because the need for cash is existential, meaning the company cannot survive without it. But a Down Round is not a good sign for future investors.

INVESTING

BUSINESS BASICS EXPLAINED SIMPLY

1.

"STOCK / SHARES"

Stock, and in plural, stocks, also known as Shares, are ownership units in a company. Each unit represents a portion of the ownership. So if you own any Stock or Share in a company, you're an owner of the company, be it a local laundromat or Apple.

Obviously, one's ownership percentage is a function of the number of Shares one own's as divided by the total number of outstanding Shares. As you can imagine, owning 10 Shares of Apple Computer gives you a very minuscule ownership percentage of Apple, while ten Shares of the local laundromat, which may only have a 100 Shares outstanding will give you a 10% ownership stake in that entire company.

But an owner is an owner, no matter how big or small, and Stock/Shares are the representation of an ownership percentage.

2.

"EQUITY"

Equity is really just a fancy name for Stock ownership, be it in the stock market (collectively known as Equities) or in a single company (called Equity or an equity holding). It represents that someone possesses an ownership percentage in a company.

Sometimes it is expressed in the number of shares owned (say, 30 or 3,000 shares), and sometimes it is expressed in a percentage ownership of the company (2% or 100% etc.). There is no limitation on the number of shares one can own, but 100% is the maximum percentage we can own.

Equity is different from Owner's Equity in that though both speak to ownership value, the second is an accounting figure primarily.

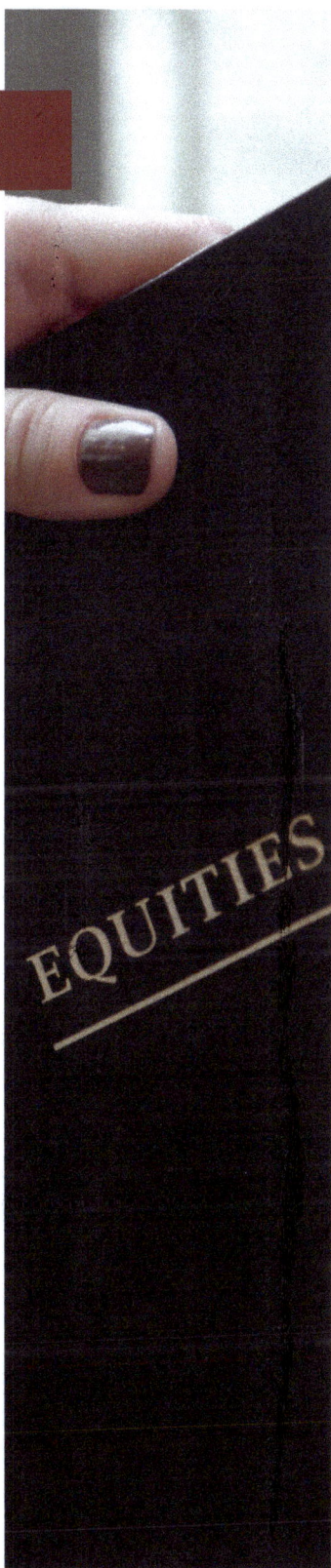

3.

"MARKET VALUE / MARKET CAPITALIZATION"

Market value and Market Capitalization are synonyms representing the total value of a company as defined in the marketplace. This is defined by a stock market, and not in an accounting sense.

It is derived by multiplying a share price per share at a given point in time against the total number of shares outstanding in investor accounts.

An example: Company XYZ has a total of 1,000,000 shares outstanding. Its share price, the cost for one share of stock, is $10 at the end of day on a stock market. So the market value / capitalization of the company is $10 Million.

4.

"OPTIONS & FUTURES"

Options and Futures are financial instruments that give the purchaser of the instruments some rights. The instruments are generally tied to stocks and other securities like commodities.

In the case of Futures, the purchaser is *obligated* to buy or sell some asset. In the case of Options, the purchaser *gets the option* to buy or sell some asset. It is this obligation or option that is the difference.

An example: One can buy a Futures contract to purchase the S&P 500 at a certain price on a certain date. A Futures contract is something that must occur. One can also buy an Options contract for the same asset, but here, the purchaser has the option to buy the S&P 500, not the obligation.

5.

"TO BE LONG SOMETHING"

To Be Long Something, most typically stocks, is when we have ownership of that something through a purchase of it. We have purchased 100 shares of Apple stock so we are long Apple stock.

Most generally, we are Long something when we believe it is going to go up in value. So in the case where we buy Apple shares, we did this because we believe that Apple shares are going to go up in value. That is, we "went" long Apple shares because we believe the shares will appreciate in value.

The vast majority of investors own shares in a company, thus are long, because they believe the stock of the company is going to go up.

6.

"TO BE SHORT SOMETHING"

In Finance, when we say that we are Short Something, it means that we believe that something is going down in value, usually stocks, and we have taken steps to create profits from this belief.

Generally with stocks, when we go short a stock, we borrow stock to sell from someone else, normally a major stock investment company, knowing we have to return this stock at a later date. The hope is that the stock drops in value so that we can purchase the stock at a lower price than we borrowed it at, return it because it was borrowed, thus making a profit.

Going Short is quite risky as something can rise in price unlimitedly, and we'll have to replenish the borrowed stock at higher price.

7.

"BULLS AND BEARS"

Bulls and Bears are nicknames for someone's position on where the price of an asset is heading. If someone believes that the price of an asset is going to go up, that person is a Bull on that something. If someone believes that the price of an asset is going to go down, that person is a Bear on that asset.

We often also use the adjectives Bullish and Bearish to describe the person who has an opinion on the price of an asset.

An easy way to remember the meaning of the two words is to think of how each animal attacks. A Bull rears upward when it attacks and a Bear attacks downward when it attacks.

8.

"BONDS"

Bonds are a financial instrument that act as a loan from someone to a company, government or other entity such as certain agencies. Essentially, a company sells a Bond to the public, getting the proceeds from that sale in cash to be used for the corporate purposes they decide.

In return, the purchasers of the Bonds get a risky guarantee that they will receive back the money lent to the company plus something to make it worthwhile. The money returned back is the Principal. The extra that makes the loan worthwhile is known as Interest.

Bonds carry varying rates of interest based on their risk, which is an assessment of the company's ability to pay back the Principal and make the Interest payments.

9.

"CALL OPTION"

A Call Option is a financial instrument that one can buy that allows the buyer the option to *buy* an asset, most commonly stocks. A Call Option gives one the option to buy a stock at a specific price on a given day. With stock, one option controls 100 shares.

An example. I believe the price of Apple stock which is now $100 will go to $200. To increase my possible success, I buy an option that allows me to get 100 shares of Apple at $100 dated 3 months from today. My hope in buying a Call Option on Apple at $100 is that its price is something higher in 3 months.

Options are risky, because if the stock doesn't go up in price, the option will expire worthless and all the investment will be lost.

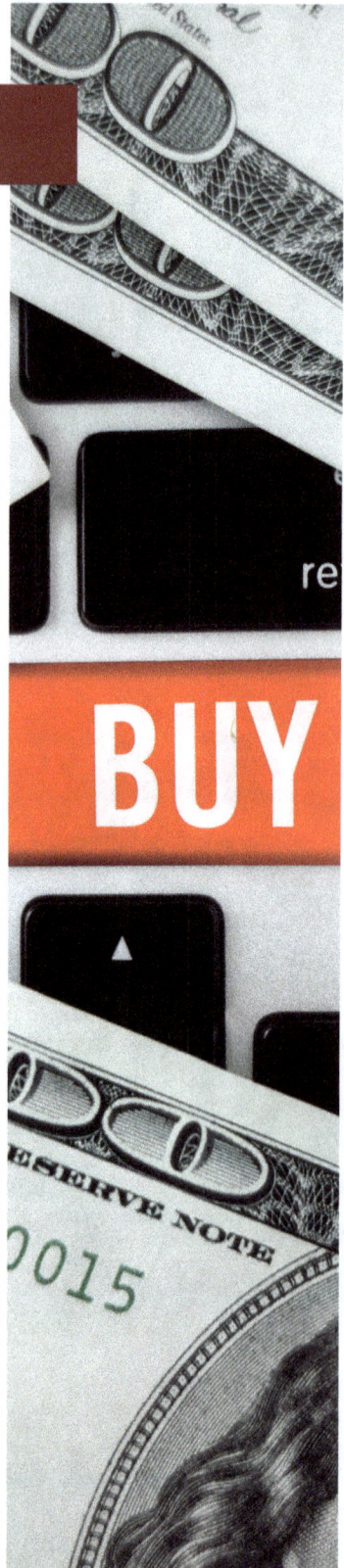

10.

"PUT OPTION"

A Put Option is a financial instrument that one can buy that allows the buyer the option to sell an asset, most commonly stocks. A Put Option gives one the option to sell a stock at a specific price on a given day. With stock, one option controls 100 shares.

An example. I believe the price of Apple stock which is now $200 will go to $100. To increase my possible profit, I buy an option that allows me to sell 100 shares of Apple at $200 three months from today. The hope is the price of Apple drops to $100, and now I have the option to sell it at $200.

Put Options are risky, because if the stock doesn't go down in price, the option will expire worthless and all the investment will be lost.

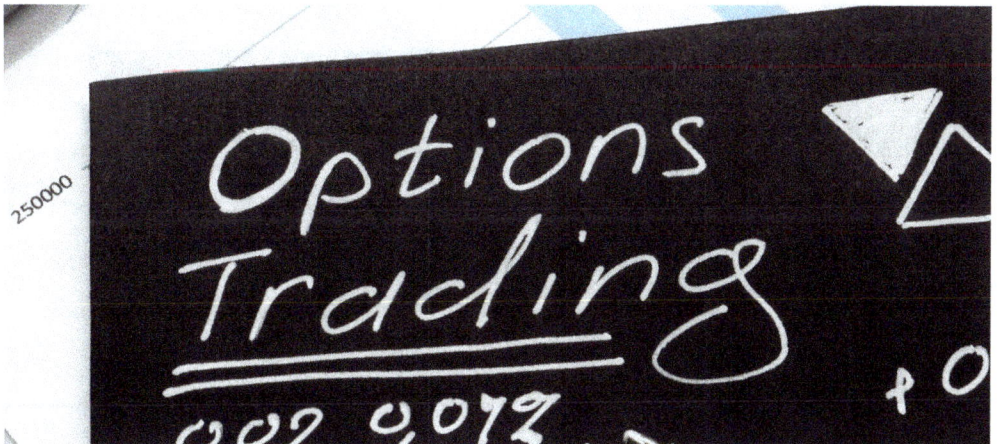

11.

"DURATION"

Duration is a measurement of the weighted average time that cashflows are received from some asset. Various assets pay different cashflows to the owner of the asset. These cash flows often are received in different periods. Duration measures, as a weighted average, how long the cashflows are received.

An example: I buy a bond that comes due in 5 years from today. The cashflows that I'll receive will be Interest for five years then I will receive back the
Principal on the bond. Duration will measure the weighted average in years of the cashflows coming to me. $500 in Interest each year, then $5,000 returned in the end.

In general, an investor wants to shorten their duration when interests are rising, and lengthen their duration when interest rates are falling.

12.

"DIVIDENDS"

Most simply, Dividends are payments made by a company to the shareholders of that company. The Dividends are made from the excess cash the company has in reserve, and usually are only paid when the reserves are so sufficient that the company cannot effectively use the excess cash to grow the business.

Many fast-growing companies, like technology companies, do not pay a Dividend as the company has what it believes are excellent projects to invest their cash in, projects that will fund future growth. However, oftentimes, older companies in slower growing industries, like banks or industrial companies, don't have enough growth projects to invest in so they return the excess cash the business generates. Dividends can be paid, monthly, quarterly or annually. A company is not obligated to pay dividends.

13.

"STOCK SPLIT"

From time to time, a public company trading on a stock exchange will decide to do a Stock Split, essentially cutting their stock price while giving current shareholders more shares to compensate for the cutting of their stock price. In the end, after the cutting of price and the suppling of shares, the shareholders is in exactly the same position of value as before these moves. Clearer, Stock Splits do NOT create any value for the shareholders.

However, many times, stocks do rise in value in response to the announcement of a Stock Split. Generally it is believed that the lowering of the stock increases the number of potential investors in a stock, since the market size has grown and this drives interest in the stock. This is generally tied to companies with a stock price that is very high in a per share basis.

14.

"TAX LOSS HARVESTING"

In the United States, we pay taxes on Capital gains, the difference between what we bought an asset at and what we sold the asset for, assuming it's a positive difference. If we bought a stock for $100 and we sold it for $200, there is a capital gain of $100 and we must pay taxes on it. Sometimes we have a Capital loss where we bought it for $200 and we sold it for $100. We are allowed to write off our losses against our gains to minimize our taxable income, and then thereafter our tax payments.

So at the end of each year, good investors do Tax Loss Harvesting, where they sell stocks that have losses in to offset against stock sales with gains. This lowers their taxable income, ultimately lowering their tax payments.

15.

"INVESTMENT HORIZON"

Investment Horizon is a key metric when developing one's profile for making investing decisions. It stands for how long an investor has the capacity to remain invested in their investments, and it adjusts over time.

For example, a young person of 25 years old, when developing an investment portfolio for retirement, has an investment horizon of at least 40 years, the difference between 25 and retirement age. A retired person at the age of 70 has a much shorter investment horizon, say five to 10 years, as their life expectancy would be typically much shorter and thus their investing period is much more limited.

One should think of their investment horizon when making decisions about Investments especially related to retirement.

16.

"RISK PROFILE / RISK TOLERANCE"

Along with Investment Horizon, Risk Tolerance, also known as one's Risk Profile, is a metric that measures one's ability to withstand risk and "problematic events" with their investment portfolio. In this case, problematic events can be defined as a loss of a substantial portion or all of invested capital in an asset purchased for investment.

Those people with less Risk Tolerance should make sure to invest in certain asset classes that by definition come with lower risk such as government bonds. Those people with a higher Risk Tolerance can be more comfortable investing in assets that have a greater chance of not succeeding such as speculative stocks and startups.

17.

"INVESTOR PROFILE"

One's Investor Profile is an analysis and study of an investor's Risk Tolerance and Investment Horizon together. The Investor Profile gives insight into the nature of the investor's goals and objectives when it comes to investing.

The analysis breaks down into four quadrants: high and low Risk Tolerance, and long and short Investment Horizon.

It is extremely useful to know one's investor profile before one begins the Investment portfolio building process. One's Investment Profile generally changes over time with changes in age and readily investable cash amounts.

18.

"REALIZED / UNREALIZED GAINS (PROFITS)"

In Business, generally, we do not pay taxes on profits that have not been Realized yet. What this means is, we only pay taxes on profits that exist because we have made money on an asset that we bought or created, then sold the asset, thereby creating a Realized Gain. It is the act of selling the asset with a profit that makes it Realized.

If we have a profit on an asset but we have not yet sold the asset, we say that profit is Unrealized. Unrealized profits are not taxable because we cannot know the future and we don't know if the Unrealized gains will remain in existence in the future. By selling the asset and realizing the profit, we know the profit exists and thus taxes must be paid.

19.

"STORE OF VALUE"

An asset is said to have a Store of Value when it can be priced, have that price be relatively stable, and be used as currency in some fashion for an exchange of goods. The most classic asset that acts as an example of a Store of Value is a common currency such as the United States dollar.

To explain further by way of an example, the United States dollar can be priced and is in a market everyday, its price is relatively stable over time so parties can trust its value, and it can be used for an exchange of goods easily and readily.

By contrast, Bitcoin has no Store of Value because its price is not very stable, so it would be foolish for people to use it in an exchange for goods.

20.

"GREATER FOOL THEORY"

The old adage is "That a Fool and his money are soon parted." This somewhat underpins the Greater Fool Theory, which expounds that one does not need to be right when purchasing some asset like a stock at a high price, one just needs to find a greater fool to sell the asset to later at a higher price.

This explains why asset bubbles happen and mania creeps into the price of assets like stocks during a craze. People will still buy the asset after it has increased in price tremendously and they may be right about doing so as long as they can find some greater fool to sell their product to at a later date at a higher price.

Beware not to be the last fool standing with the asset when the market crashes back down.

21.

"ASSET BUBBLES"

Asset Bubbles occur when a mania sets in for the purchasing of some asset, usually stocks in a stock market, but not always. The most famous Asset Bubble was a tulip craze in Holland in the 17th century. Yes, the plant. Tulips.

However despite the tulip fiasco, the most common Asset Bubble is either stocks on a stock market or housing prices. The 21st century created two vicious asset bubbles in its first 10 years with the internet stock market bubble in the years 1998-2001 and the housing bubble from years 2004-2007.

Each ended extremely painfully for so many lives, with savings wiped out for so many. So beware. Absurd things happen, and bad timing due to ignorance can be life-changingly painful.

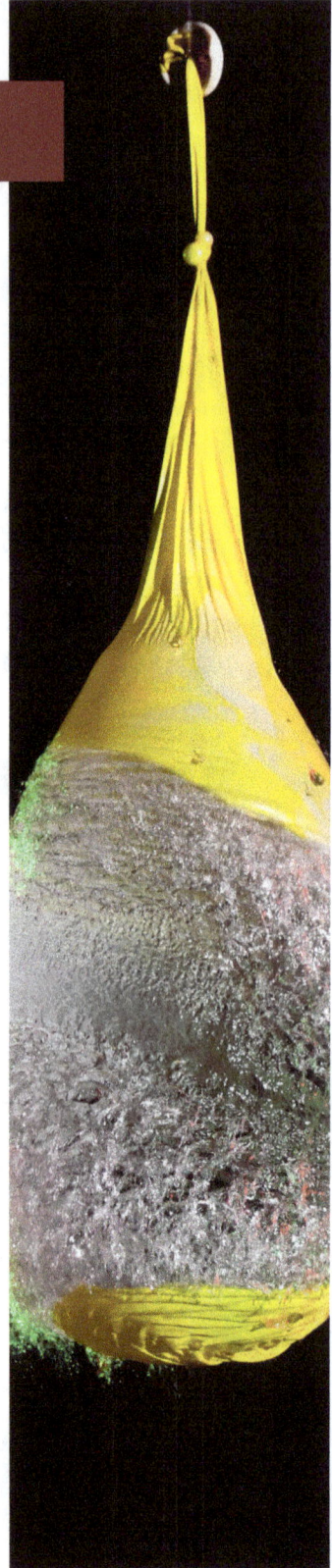

22.

"F.O.M.O"
(FEAR OF MISSING OUT)

One of the most consistent causes of asset bubbles and stock market crashes is FOMO, or Fear Of Missing Out. How it works is simple. Some asset, usually the stock market, achieves great returns over a short period of time. Those people who have not participated because they were not invested into the stock market become afraid that they will not get their share of gains, so they rush to invest.

This Fear Of Missing Out only feeds itself, as it propels stocks higher to absurd ranges, thereby drawing more people into it until it is self-fulfilling. Until it crashes.

The last people always pay the worst price because theie FOMO pushed them to enter far too late.

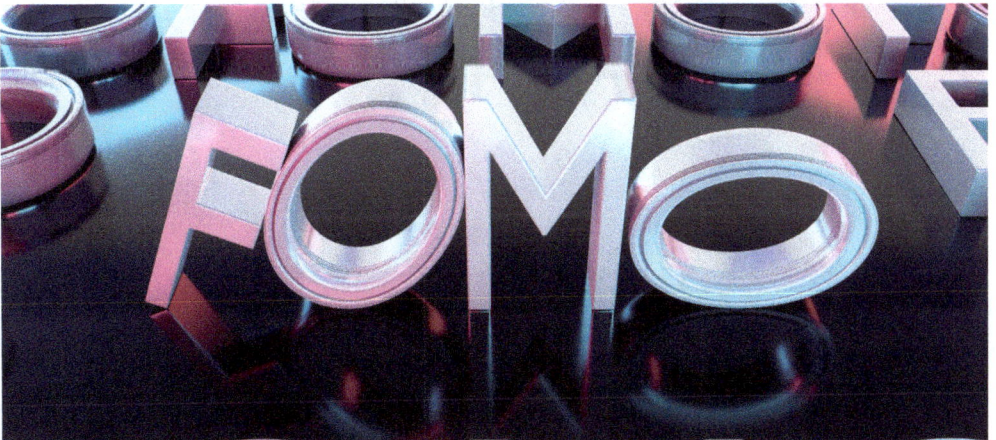

23.

"DOLLAR COST AVERAGING"

Dollar Cost Averaging is an investing approach where similar amounts are put into an investment regardless of timing or the price of the investment. Over time, it will lead an averaging of higher and lower investment prices, which will lead to solid investment returns.

As an example, imagine putting $200 into the stock market each month irrespective of the price of the stock market or what is happening in the broader investing market. Sometimes the $200 will be invested when stock prices are low, but other times it will be when stock prices are high. This generates an average investment price over time. This approach limits the attempts of investors to try to time the market (see definition).

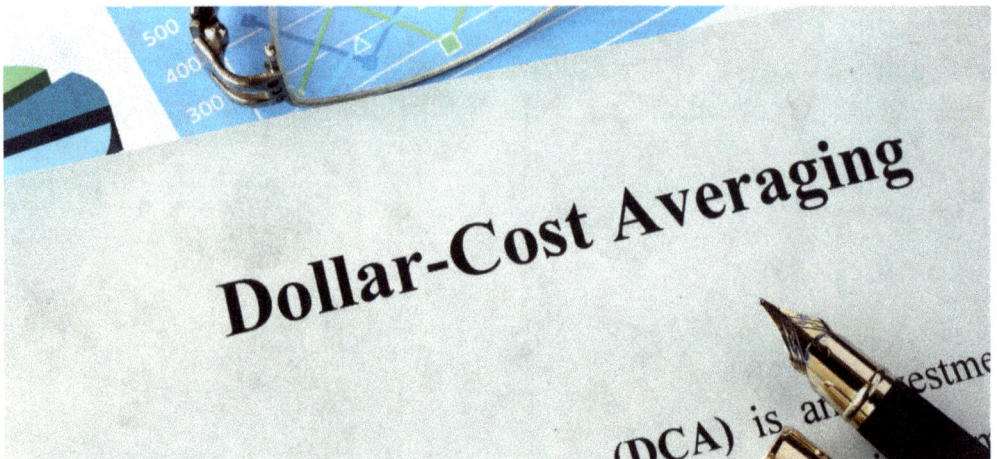

24.

"MARKET TIMING / TIMING THE MARKET"

Market Timing, aka Timing the Market, is in approach to investing that far too many new investors try but over time rarely succeed at. It is based on the belief that someone can make a decision as to when it is a good or bad time to be invested in the market. The old desire to buy low and sell high drives the belief, often mistaken, that one can time the market, buy at the right time and sell and the right time.

Studies show overwhelmingly that the vast majority of investors cannot Market Time effectively, often because it takes making two correct decisions: buying at the right time and selling it the right time. Statistically the chances of making those two decisions correctly are very small.

25.

"BUY AND HOLD STRATEGY"

Buy and Hold Strategy is an approach to investing that acknowledges it is quite difficult to know and act at the right times to buy and the right times to sell in the stock market.

This approach believes that it is better to buy a good company's stock and hold it through good times and bad in the overall market, unless the underlying story about the company has changed substantially enough.

Studies show that, despite the fact most people believe they can time the stock market, better returns are achieved with a Buy and Hold Strategy. So unless one is extremely knowledgeable and extremely focused on stock market investing, Buy and Hold is the best strategy.

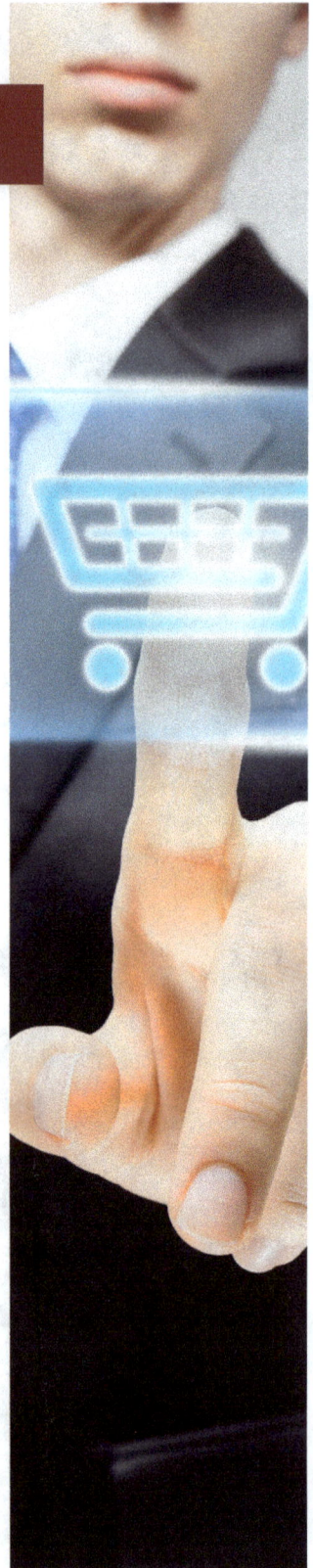

26.

"PRICE EARNINGS RATIO P.E. RATIO"

One of the most important Investment metrics in investment analysis is the Price Earnings Ratio, often abbreviated to the PE Ratio or just PE. It is a metric that relates the price of a company's stock on a stock market to the amount of earnings per share that the company has or is expecting to earn.

As an example to calculate, imagine a company earns $3 per share of stock outstanding and the company's stock is currently trading at $100. By dividing $100 by $3, we get a P.E. of 33.3. Thus this company is trading at 33 times its earning per share. The PE Ratio changes constantly as the stock price can change moment to moment on an exchange. Additionally, as companies earnings change or the forecast for them change, this also will change the PE Ratio.

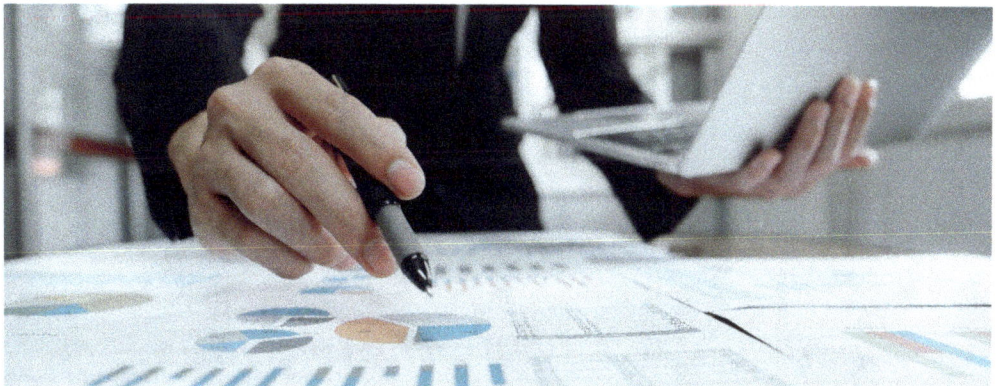

27.

"P.E.G. RATIO"

A more advanced version of the PE Ratio is the Price Earnings Growth ratio, otherwise known as the PEG ratio. This is ratio relates the PE Ratio of the company with the projected earnings growth of that company.

Let's take an example: A company has a PE Ratio of 20, which means a company is trading at 22 times its earnings per share. If the company is expected to grow its earnings at 40% per year, it has a PEG Ratio of 2.

Generally, investors like to invest in companies with a higher PEG ratio, as in some ways, it represents a good value relative to other companies with a lower PEG Ratio.

28.

"FUNDAMENTAL ANALYSIS"

One of the two different Financial Analysis approaches used to forecast individual stocks, stock markets and other tradable assets is Fundamental Analysis. This is the traditional approach most put forward by financial analysts on Wall Street.

Fundamental Analysis sounds like what it is, essentially analyzing company stocks, stock markets and other tradable assets based on the fundamentals underlying each of those assets. For stocks, it is most often Revenue, Cashflow and Profit Growth. Fundamental analysis is often a tool by which to compare different stocks and assets against each other to help foresee upcoming pricing trends.

When done most effectively, Fundamental Analysis often leads to better financial investing decisions.

29.

"TECHNICAL ANALYSIS"

One of the two different Financial Analysis approaches used to forecast individual stocks, stock markets and other tradable assets is Technical Analysis. It is a unique, somewhat obscure approach to forecasting and predicting asset movements in price based on the theory that moves in asset prices following recurring and recognizable patterns.

Its belief is that by studying those patterns and studying current movements in asset prices will offer insight and clues to the next movements. While sometimes this approach seems far-fetched or even counterintuitive, it is essential to recognize that many investors follow this approach and that it affects markets as a result.

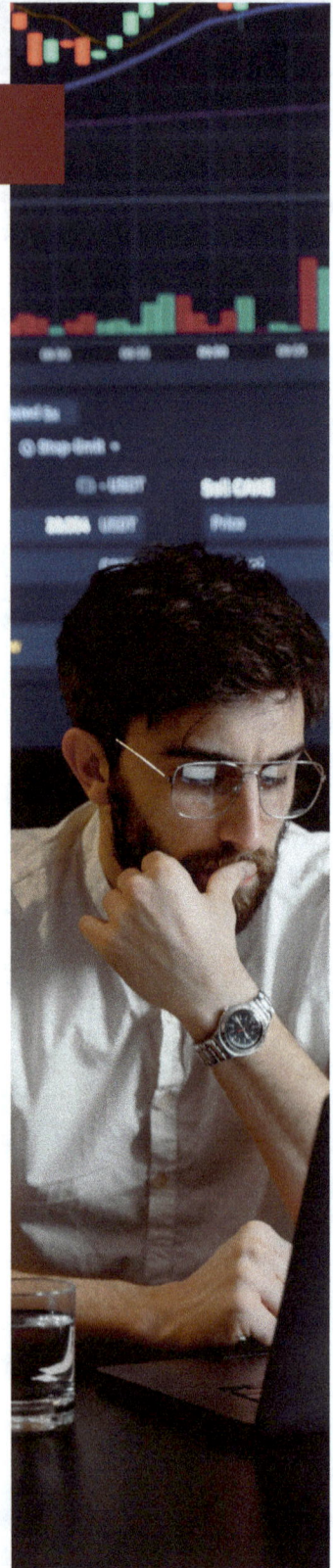

30.

"GROWTH STOCKS"

Very broadly speaking, investors often talk of stocks falling into one of two categories: Growth Stocks and Value Stocks. The main difference between the two is in the rate of growth in their earnings from year to year.

Growth Stocks are, as the name implies, those stocks that are growing their earnings at a great rate from year to year. To be considered a Growth Stock, the earnings should be growing generally in excess of 10% per year, often much more than that.

A lot of technology companies tend to fall in this category: we can often think of Facebook or Google or Amazon, which have achieved tremendous year-on-year earnings growth over a substantial, sustained period of time.

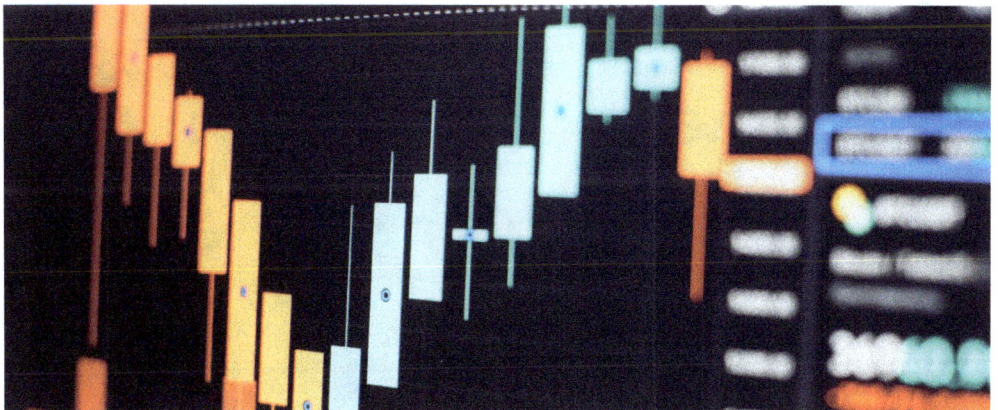

31.

"VALUE STOCKS"

Very broadly speaking, investors often talk of stocks falling into one of two categories: Growth Stocks and Value Stocks. The main difference between the two is in the rate of growth in their earnings from year to year.

Value Stocks are those stocks whose earnings are growing at a slow rate from year to year, and sometimes barely at all. They are called Value Stocks because they trade at a low multiple of earnings, and can offer great value because of this low PE multiple.

This category of stocks is characterized by many old-line industries such as banks, heavy equipment companies and utilities. That is companies whose high growth days are mostly behind them. They often pay a nice dividend.

32.

"GOVERNMENT BONDS"

Government Bonds are a large category of bonds issued by a government, most usually the Federal government of a country. In essence, it a loan to the government issuing the bond. These bonds most often carry an interest rate and will make Principal and Interest payments based on the amount of the bond held by the bondholder.

Government Bonds come in different forms based on their time until its expiration, the day it will return the Principal of the bond. They come in a range of expiration dates from very short term (1 to 3 months) to very long term (30 years). The Principal and Interest of the bonds are guaranteed by what is known as "the full faith and credit" of the issuing institution, in this case, the federal government, which is guaranteeing repayment.

33.

"TREASURY BILLS / NOTES / BONDS"

This category of debt instruments, Treasury Bills, Notes and Bonds are in essence governmental bonds issued by a Federal government. They carry Principal and Interest payments and their repayments are guaranteed by the Federal government.

The only difference between Treasury Bills, Treasury Notes and Treasury Bonds is the time frame of the loan to the government. Treasury Bills are udebt instruments of less than two years. Treasury Notes are debt instruments of between two and 10 years. Treasury Bonds are debt instruments of 10 years or greater. The longest Treasury Bond the US government issues is currently the 30 year bond. There is talk of a 50 year bond, but it has never been issued.

34.

"THE FEDERAL RESERVE BANK AND SYSTEM"

The Federal Reserve Bank and its system of subordinate Banks beneath it, acts as the bank of the United States of America without technically being the bank of the United States. It handles the banking functions for the Federal government and sets short-term interest rate policies as an act of its role in setting what is known Monetary Policy, which it controls to a certain tangible degree.

The Federal Reserve Bank and its system of banks support and regulate the larger banking system of which almost all public and private banks are a part. "The Fed" as it is known, has two goals mandated by Congress: One is maximizing employment, and the other is price stability.

35.

"MONEY MARKET FUND"

A Money Market Fund is a type of mutual fund that invests specifically in short-term assets, most often very short-term government and municipal bonds with an expiration of less than two years. It is a type of fund that is extremely riskless because of the nature of the holdings in the funds, that is short-term government bonds which are secured by the US government.

Many times the cash balance in investment accounts, and even cash balances in bank accounts will be invested in Money Market Funds so that the cash balance can generate some tangible financial return, if not a overwhelmingly great one, over time.

36.

"MUNICIPAL BONDS"

Municipal Bonds are governmental debt instruments issued by a municipal authority such as a state, a city, a township and even a municipal taxing authority, like a highway toll authority. Like other governmental bonds, Municipal Bonds pay interest and return the Principal borrowed and the payments and repayment are backed by the full faith and credit of the issuing Municipal authority.

While there are several different variations of Municipal Bonds—those supported on tax revenues, on toll revenues or a combination of both—it is important to note that Municipal Bonds, often shortened in the trade to Muni Bonds, are riskier than Federal government bonds, and in fact, extremely few have defaulted. However equally important to note Municipal Bonds are usually triple tax free, meaning the interest one receives is not taxed on any level, city, state or federal, which adds to their popularity.

Municipal Building

POLICE

37.

"FED FUNDS RATE"

The Federal Funds Rate, also known as the Fed Funds Rate, is the interest rate that the Federal Reserve Bank of the United States (The Fed) charges its member banks for loans the banks take with the Federal Reserve. Member Banks are the largest Global banks in the world with operations in the United States.

The Federal Reserve sets the Fed Funds Rate, and this rate acts in some manner as a basis for most other interests rates that exist. The Fed uses the Fed Funds Rate to attempt to affect the United States economy, in theory slowing the economy by raising the rate, or conversely, lowering the rate in an attempt to expand or grow the economy. As the Fed changes the rate, more or less loans are made at higher or lower interest rates, and thus business activities are affected.

38.

"ASSETS UNDER MANAGEMENT (AUM)"

Assets Under Management, abbreviated as AUM, is a common term by which to measure the size in dollars of various financial funds, companies or management firms. It is a calculation of all the assets in dollar terms that is being managed by whichever entity it is describing. The assets can include all financial instruments such as stocks, bonds, cash, real estate, commodities, cryptocurrency, etc.

Many companies or Financial Management entities will use Assets Under Management as a marketing tool to express their impressive size hoping to communicate a sense of acceptance and institutional support. Though AUM does connote size, it doesn't necessarily correspond with success.

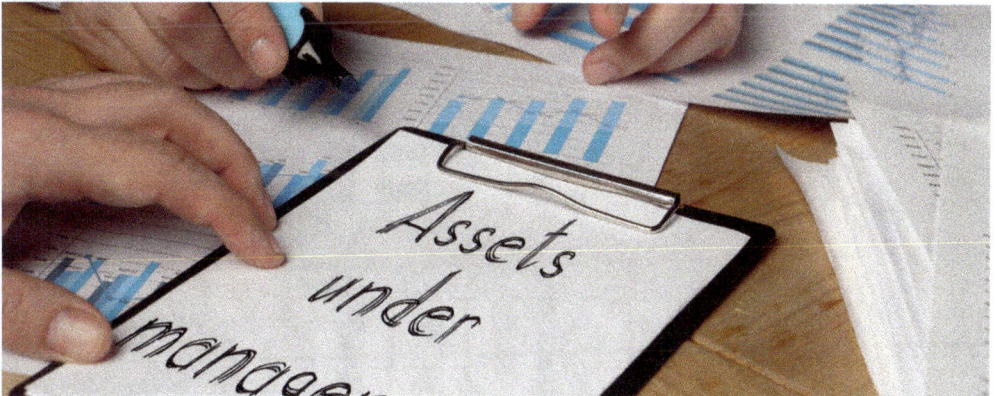

39.

"MORTGAGE BACKED SECURITIES"

Mortgage-Backed Securities (MBS) are a type of debt/bond instruments that are made up of a large amalgam of underlying mortgages which have been grouped together and sold as one debt instrument. The bond elements themselves (by that I mean the payment of interest and repayment of principal) are backed by the mortgage payments of the underlying mortgages supporting the grouping in the bond.

Mortgage-Backed securities are riskier than government securities, as we found out during the Financial Crisis of 2007-09, because they are not backed by the US government. However, on the whole over time, they have been a fine investment as a percentage of one's investment holdings.

40.

"TALKING YOUR OWN BOOK"

Something we must be wary of when watching TV pundits on stock news channels is them Talking Their Own Book. This is when someone touts their own holdings, say stocks that they own, recommending others purchase what they already have a financial position in. This is Talking Your Own Book.

It is important to recognize that people have biases, and often their biases are influenced by where they have invested their own money. Often times you will hear financial advisors, as a sort of disclaimer, mention that they are Talking Their Own Book, which they should do. It means that they are recommending something that they have a financial interest in.

ACCOUNTING

BUSINESS BASICS EXPLAINED SIMPLY

1.

"REVENUE, TOTAL & GROSS"

Revenue is the business term for Sales and can be used interchangeably with the word Sales. When we make a sale, that is selling (giving someone or a business a good or service for a price), we create Revenue. Sales and Revenue are synonyms in a financial sense, with different companies and different industries using them interchangeably as is typical to that company or industry.

Total Revenue, also known as Gross Revenue, is the sum of all sales that are made in a given period. We calculate Gross Revenue by adding up all the sales of all the products and services sold, regardless of the type or nature of the good or service sold. One can calculate Gross Revenue of a given product or service, or one can calculate Total Revenue across a business.

2.

"VARIABLE EXPENSES"

Variable Expenses are those expenses that vary specifically with revenue. They are defined differently than fixed expenses which do not vary with revenue.

Examples: If we had a business that sold pencils, each time we sold one pencil, we would have a cost for the eraser, the graphite inside, the wood outside and the metal holding the eraser to the wood. Each sale costs us every one of those elements. So these costs vary with the revenue made. As does wrapping, boxes, shipping, etc.

Differently, each sale of a pencil will not increase our rent expense, salaries, insurance etc. We call these expenses 'fixed' because they do not vary with each unit sold of revenue.

3.

"COSTS OF GOODS SOLD (COGS)"

Costs of Goods sold is a version of looking at Variable expenses, more specifically designed for those companies that are selling a product. Service-providing companies, while they offer a good, more traditionally look at a Variable expenses categorization.

As you can imagine, COGS are those expenses tied directly to the product sold and the costs that increase as a unit of product sold increases. For example, with a shoe company, the costs are the leather of the shoe, the rubber for the sole, the laces, the boxing and wrapping and other things directly tied to the product itself. As each unit of a product is sold, the cost of goods sold increase.

State Fees

F

Cost of wnership

Mc

Depreciation

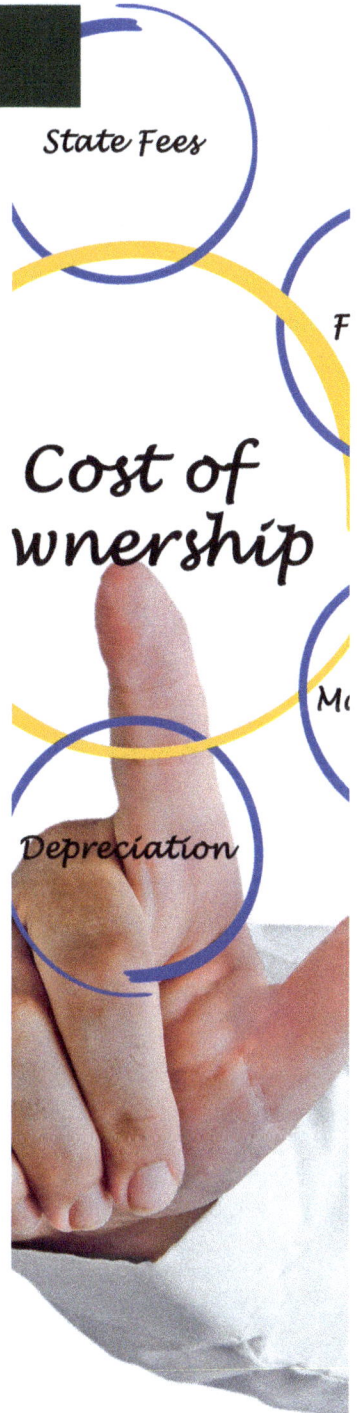

4.

"FIXED EXPENSES"

Fixed Expenses are those expenses that do not vary specifically with revenue. That is to say that an additional unit of sales does not increase these types of expenses.

Put even clearer, the costs associated with each sale of our product will not increase our expenses that are fixed, such as rent expense, salaries, insurance, etc. For this reason specifically, we call these expenses 'fixed' because they do not vary with each unit sold of revenue.

Examples: If we had a business most fixed expenses categories for all businesses are Salaries and Benefits, Marketing, Rent, Insurance, Office Management Supplies, Utilities, etc.

5.

"T & E"

In long form, T&E stands for Travel and Entertainment expenses. These expenses are wide-ranging and are very often essential for the running of the business and even increasing sales. Often they go by the nickname T&E.

They include Airfare, Car Expenses, Hotels, Train and Subway fares, and even Business Meals and Entertainment events provided those are with clients or purchased for employees when the team is working through lunch or dinner hour.

Pay attention here! The misuse and even abuse of the these expenses are one of the areas that most lead to IRS tax audits. So only write-off legitimate Business expenses.

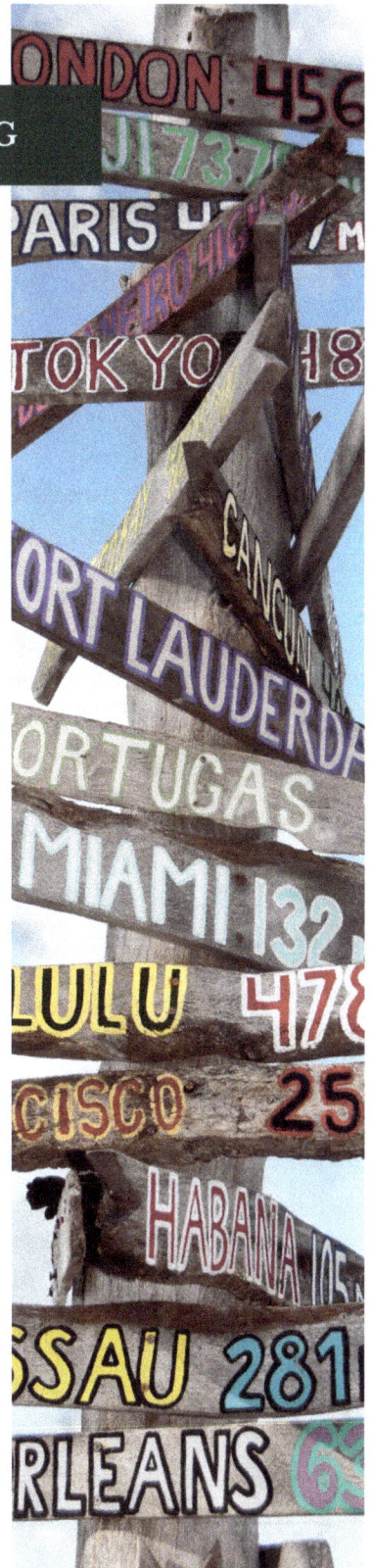

6.

"NET REVENUE"

Net Revenue is the total revenue number produced subtracted by some amount. This is the general meaning of 'Net' in that it removes some amount from a total. With Net Revenue, oftentimes it is Total Revenue minus a figure like returned sales or reimbursed expenses. Here, the total amount of returned sales is subtracted from the Total Revenue to get a Net Revenue figure.

The goal with calculating Net Revenue is to get to a truer figure about how a company is doing by subtracting out items that artificially inflate the Total Revenue figure. In some business scenarios, returns of sales can be very substantial with credits making up a significant percentage of Total Revenue. The Net Revenue figure is the more true figure for assessing sales success or disappoinment in a period.

7.

"DEBT"

Debt is the name business gives to monies owed to someone or something like a bank or other lending institution. Debt is a part of the Total Liabilities category. When a business takes a loan, either short-term or long or both, we collectively refer to this amount outstanding and needed to be repaid as Debt.

Debt is not necessarily a bad thing for a business to have, but too much of it is difficult to manage as eventually we have to pay back to the lender both the Principal and Interest on the Principal (the amount we borrowed). This can adversely effect the cash flow of a company especially if there is too much cash being utilized for payments.

So managing total debt is essential for the long-term success of a business.

107

8.

"DEPRECIATION / AMORTIZATION"

Depreciation is an expense that concerns that aging of tangible, physical assets, and amortization is an expense of aging concerning intangible assets like trademarks.

In accounting, for tax purposes, the costs of purchasing assets are often depreciated/amortized over a period of time, and not all at once in total. Depreciation is the amount that is expensed in a given period. For example: A computer costs $3,000 and has a useful life of three years. The Depreciation cost of this asset is $1,000 a year for three years even though the actual cash outflow was $3,000 total.

There are multiple ways of depreciating/amortizing assets, which can effect total Depreciation expense and profits.

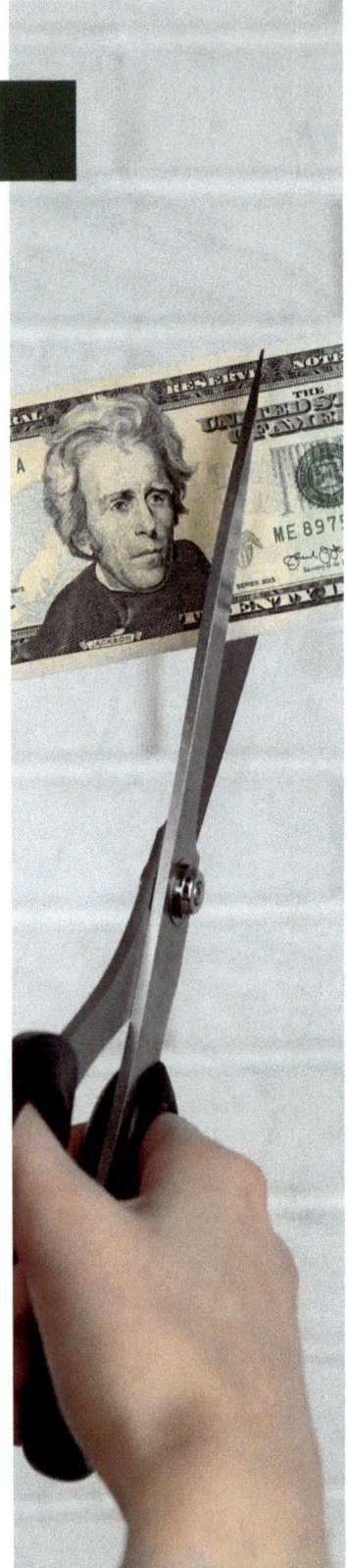

9.

"ACCUMULATED DEPRECIATION"

As assets are depreciated over periods of time, Accumulated Depreciation is the total sum of depreciation that has occurred since the beginning when Depreciation started.

As an example, imagine a computer which costs $3,000 and is being depreciated over three years, its useful life. Thus, the depreciation expense is $1,000 a year, and after two years of this, the Accumulated Depreciation is $2,000.

In this scenario, $1,000 is the remaining asset value for the computer. When total Accumulated Depreciation equals the original cost of the asset, the asset has no value on the Balance Sheet.

10.

"ASSETS"

To make it very simple, an asset is something that has value. It is generally something that can be sold at some price to a buyer outside the company. The most classic examples in business are cash in a bank account, inventory of products, monies owed to the company in the form of a loan to someone, or monies owed to the company for payment of sales to them (Accounts Receivable defined in coming pages).

Assets are one of the three main sections of the Balance Sheet financial statement. The ratio of assets to various things like liabilities or equity (defined on other pages here) are key metrics that investors and bankers use to decide on the credit or investing worthiness of a company.

11.

"LIABILITIES"

Somewhat different to the definition in regular life, Liabilities in business mean that money is owed to someone or something. Liabilities is a broad category that can include credit card loans, long-term bank loans, bond payments to investors, and even monies to product or service providers called Accounts Payables.

Liabilities represents one of the three main sections of the Balance Sheet financial statement, and is a key figure in deciding the financial health of a company. Companies with too many Liabilities as compared with their assets or equity are often in serious financial trouble and a risk for both lenders and providers to do Business with.

12.

"OWNER'S EQUITY"

Owner's Equity is one of the main three sections of a Balance Sheet analysis, and it represents the value of the business at least as far as the Balance Sheet is concerned. It represents the Net worth of a business in its most basic form. It is calculated by subtracting the total Liabilities of the company from the total assets of the company.

Though some slight differences can exist in certain circumstances, essentially the terms Owner's Equity and Book Value are synonyms and can be used interchangeably. Book Value is usually used in an investment context. Owner's Equity is generally used more in the context of accounting and tax filing.

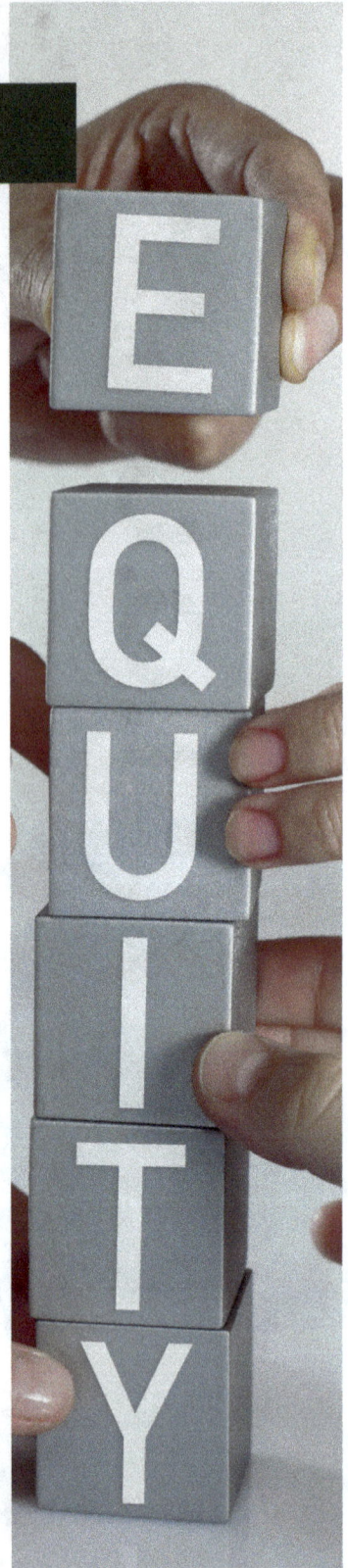

13.

"BOOK VALUE"

Book Value, for the most part, is another way of saying Owner's Equity. Thus it is defined similarly as the difference between the value of the assets as calculated on the Balance Sheet and the total Liabilities calculated on the Balance Sheet. Hence its name, it's the value of the company "on the books."

It's important to understand that Book Value is a metric rarely used to value companies, and does not truly represent the value of a company for purchase or stock valuation purposes. Because most companies are worth more than their Book Value as intangible assets like brand equity (defined elsewhere) can be worth even more than the Book Value as calculated on the Balance sheet.

Think of the value of certain brands like Apple or Coca Cola. The loyalty they inspire is invaluable, but it is not technically valued in a Book Value calculation.

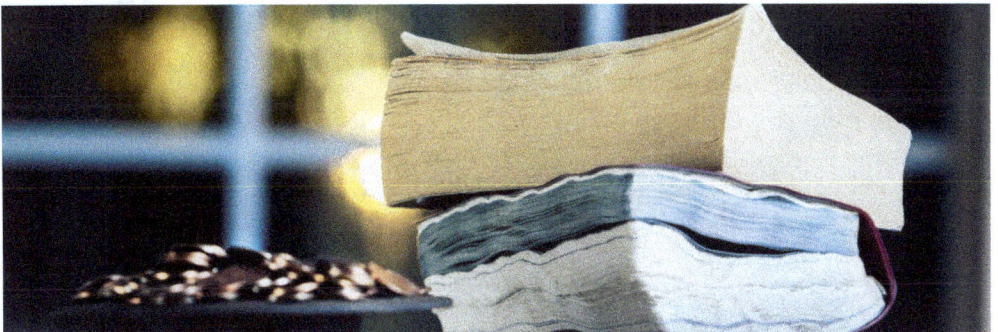

14.

"INVENTORY"

Inventory is a term that describes the stockpiles of a company's specific products that it sells. Inventory can be spoken of as a company total, when a company offers several products for sale, or as an individual total of an individual product.

For example, Apple computers will have a total Inventory number, which represents the value of all its products in Inventory. It will also have an Inventory number for a specific product like iPhones, even calculated by each series of phones. Companies also may keep Inventory of raw materials and parts.

Inventory can be described either in total dollar terms or total unit terms depending what exactly one is looking to analyze. It can also include parts and supplies.

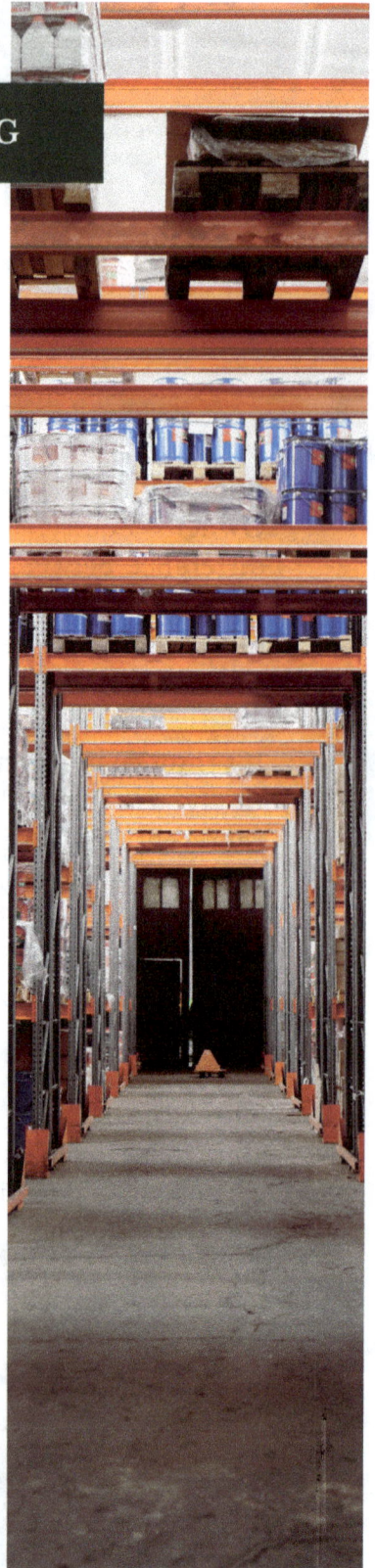

15.

THE 3 FINANCIAL STATEMENTS: "INCOME STATEMENT"

Also known as the Profit and Loss Statement interchangeably, the Income Statement is one of the three major financial statements that all companies produce from your small company to Apple computers.

This statement captures the profitability (or loss) of the company over some specific defined period of time. An Income Statement can be for a month, a quarter, annually or any other designed period. This is in contrast with a Balance Sheet, which is at a specific point in time.

Specifically, the format is a showing of revenue minus expenses which produces a profit-defining result for that period of time.

115

16.

THE 3 FINANCIAL STATEMENTS:
"BALANCE SHEET"

The Balance Sheet of a company is one of three major financial statements that all companies produce. It is essentially a Net Worth analysis of a company, showing a value on paper of what a company is worth, as well as outlining other key performance indicators.

The main analysis is a comparison of the assets of the companies to the Liabilities of the company. The difference between these two categories is known as Owner's Equity, which is a value of the company in a certain sense. In the equation, the assets of the company must equal the value of the Liabilities of the company plus its current Owner's Equity.

116

17.

THE 3 FINANCIAL STATEMENTS:
"THE CASH FLOW STATEMENT"

The least well-known of the main financial statements, but in some ways the most important, is the Cash Flow Statement, which tracks cash specifically.

In general, there are three ways Businesses generate cash. One is from its operations, the second is from investments made in assets outside the company, the third is cash from investments made by outsiders into the company. This schedule tracks the net effect, either positive or negative, of each driver of cash in the Business.

Just the fact that this analysis is one of the main schedules completed for all Business underscores how important cash is to Businesses.

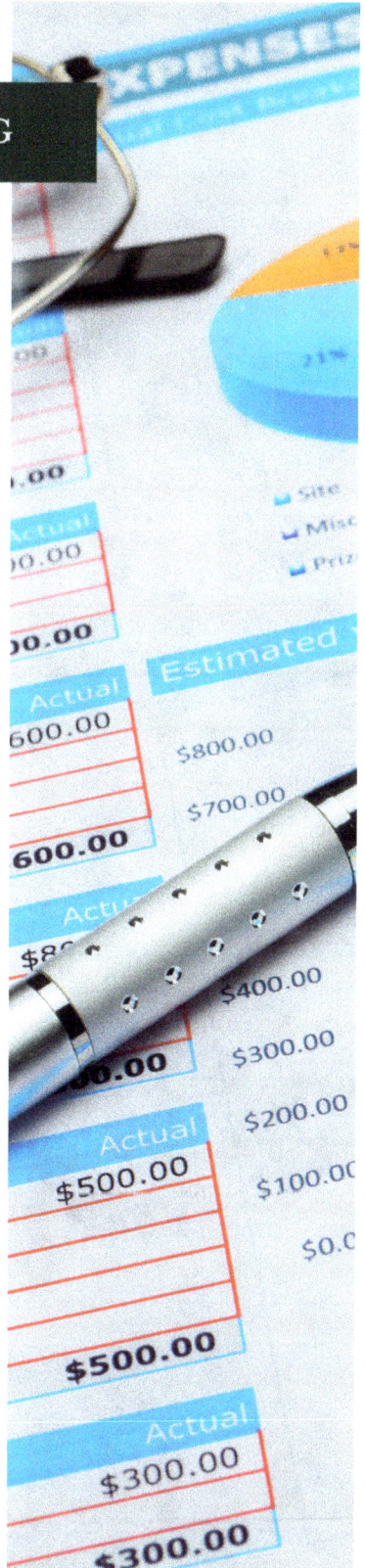

18.

"ACCOUNTS RECEIVABLE"

Accounts Receivable, or sometimes just Receivables, are a function of accrual accounting. An Account Receivable occurs when a sale has been made, but payment has not yet been received from the client. The amount that has not been received is the receivable, and it is booked with other receivables in the Accounts Receivable category.

In business, Accounts Receivable are considered an asset as they represent expected future cash payments. It is important to track Accounts Receivable to ensure that money owed is eventually paid. Sometimes it is even possible to sell receivables to a third party who pay you for them, but who will eventually receive the money in your place.

19.

"ACCOUNTS PAYABLE"

Accounts Payable, or sometimes just Payables, are a function of accrual accounting. An Account Payable occurs when an expense has been incurred, but payment has not yet been made to the from the provider. The amount that has not been paid is the payable, and it is booked with other payables in the Accounts Payable category.

In Business, accounts payable are a liability as they represent expected future cash outlays that need to be made. Without payment, vendors may stop service.

It is important to track Accounts Payable to ensure that money owed to vendors is eventually paid and their growth is managed.

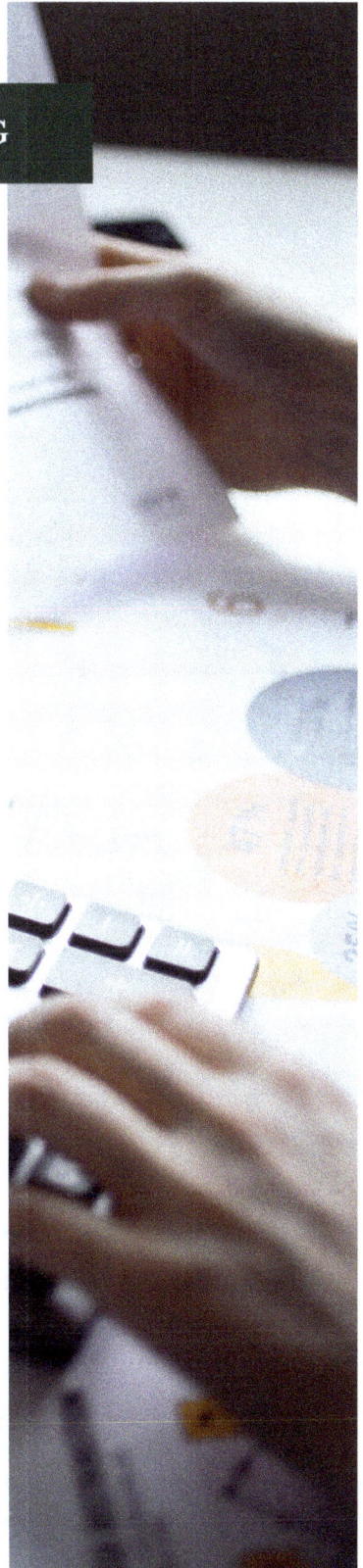

20.

"GOODWILL"

In business there are assets, and even whole companies, that are worth more than their book value carried on the company's balance sheet. Goodwill is the name given to the excess value above the calculated book value.

The most common usage is the difference between the value of a company in the marketplace versus the book value of the company on the balance sheet of the company. Book Value is the difference in value between a company's assets minus its Liabilities. The marketplace value of a company is defined by its total outstanding shares times its stock price.

If a company's Book Value is one million dollars, but its value in the marketplace is three million dollars, the two million dollar difference between the two is Goodwill.

21.

"ACCRUAL ACCOUNTING"

Accounting for businesses is generally completed in one of two fashions, either on a Cash basis or an Accrual basis. Accrual Accounting is based on accounting for things in the period that they happened as opposed to Cash Accounting, which is based on accounting for things when cash is affected. This is true for money going in or out.

An example: A sale is made this month but payment will not be received until next month. In Accrual Accounting, you measure the sale as made this month; in Cash Accounting, the sale is measured when the actual cash is received, be it next month, four months from now or whenever it comes in.

This applies to both revenue and expenses. If you incur an expense this month, it is measured this month even if you don't pay it for three months.

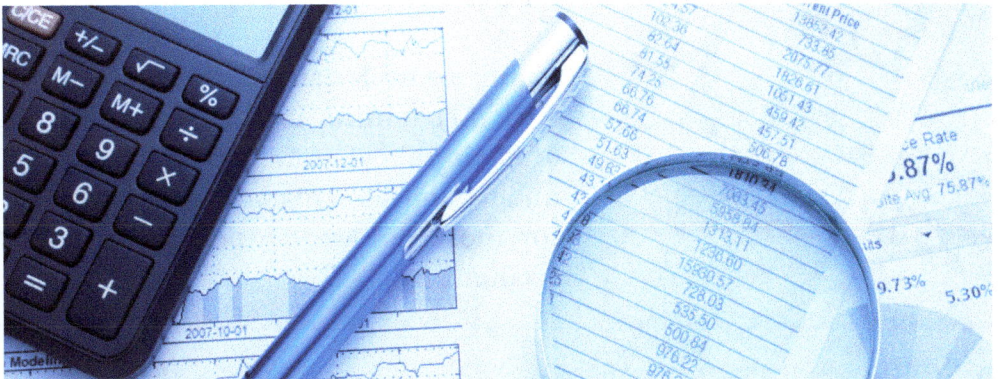

22.

"CASH ACCOUNTING"

As opposed to Accrual Accounting, Cash Accounting is more simple to understand and implement in a Small Business.

Cash Accounting treats are entries that affect a company's financial statements on the day that they actual hit the bank statement. If you make a sale on October 1st, but don't receive the payment until November 30th, the Cash Accounting of this payment is on November 30th as opposed to Accrual Accounting, where the payment would be accounted for on October 1st.

Again, most Small Businesses use Cash Accounting in the beginning of their lifecycle as it is easier to understand and manage especially for those not very experienced in accounting.

123

23.

"NET INCOME"

Net Income is the final profitability metric especially for publicly-traded companies on stock exchanges. It represents profitability after all expenses are deducted from its gross margin including fixed expenses, taxes, interest, Depreciation and Amortization.

Most very mature companies are judged by this metric of Net Income, often times also called short form Earnings. Most companies on a stock exchange are evaluated on a Net Income basis, and the most important metric existing for evaluating them is known as Earning per share, which is the total Earnings in some given period divided by the total number of shares outstanding.

24.

"OVERHEAD"

Often also called fixed expenses or fixed overhead, Overhead are those expenses that reoccur on a monthly basis, and are not tied to revenue generation. Like its synonym fixed expenses, it is the basis of a break-even analysis.

In most small businesses, monthly Overhead is most usually rent, salaries and benefits, insurance, utilities such as Internet and telephone expenses, and office expenditures among others. It is this Overhead that the company must generate enough gross margin to cover on a monthly basis to be profitable.

In small businesses, and even all businesses, it is advisable to keep monthly Overhead as low as possible, especially in the beginning of venture. It drains cash and risks future existence as a result.

25.

"CAPITAL EXPENDITURES"

Capital Expenditures, shortened to CapEx, is money that a business spends on fixed assets that have a long-term useful life. The biggest differentiation here between Capital Expenditures and other expenses is that their use happens over a long period of time usually several years as opposed to only a month or two, as is the case with normal expenses.

As an example, think of a computer which has a useful life of five years. Now in comparison, think of printer paper which gets used in a month. In business we view the long-term fixed asset purchase as an expense to be depreciated over time because it can unfairly affect financial results if expensed in only one monthly period.

26.

"LEASEHOLD IMPROVEMENTS"

Leasehold Improvements are investments that one makes to a location owned or rented, or most commonly in Business, a place of work like an office or a warehouse, to improve or augment its value. These investments are things that have a long-term useful life and are depreciated over time like other fixed assets purchases.

In Small Businesses, common Leasehold Improvements usually include painting and building fixtures for an office location, putting up walls and other useful structures in factories and warehouses.

Sometimes landlords will make these investments on rental properties as an inducement for tenants to rent or continue renting a location.

27.

"SALVAGE OR RESIDUAL VALUE"

When a company has purchased an asset and depreciated it on its books over its useful life, sometimes that asset still has some value for which it can be sold. In Business the value that remains is known as either the Salvage Value or the Residual Value.

As an example, a company buys a machine which has a useful life of three years which it depreciated appropriately in its accounting. If after the three years its full legal depreciation has been completed, the machine still has value as represented by the fact that it can be sold to someone for something, that value, the Salvage/Residual Value can be accounted for.

28.

"BAD DEBT EXPENSE"

Sadly in Business, sometimes we sell our products on credit for future payment to customers who in the end do not pay the bill. In many cases, the Business has incurred expenses by sending these lousy customers our product or completing services for them, and in the instances where the bill or Accounts Receivable are not paid, ultimately the business must accept the fact that payment will not come. We call the lost revenue, Bad Debt Expense.

The only benefit to a non-payment which becomes a Bad Debt Expense, is that a business can write off the expense, thereby lowering their profit and paying less taxes. Otherwise, it's a crappy situation that reminds one to be careful on giving sales credit to unworthy or unproven customers.

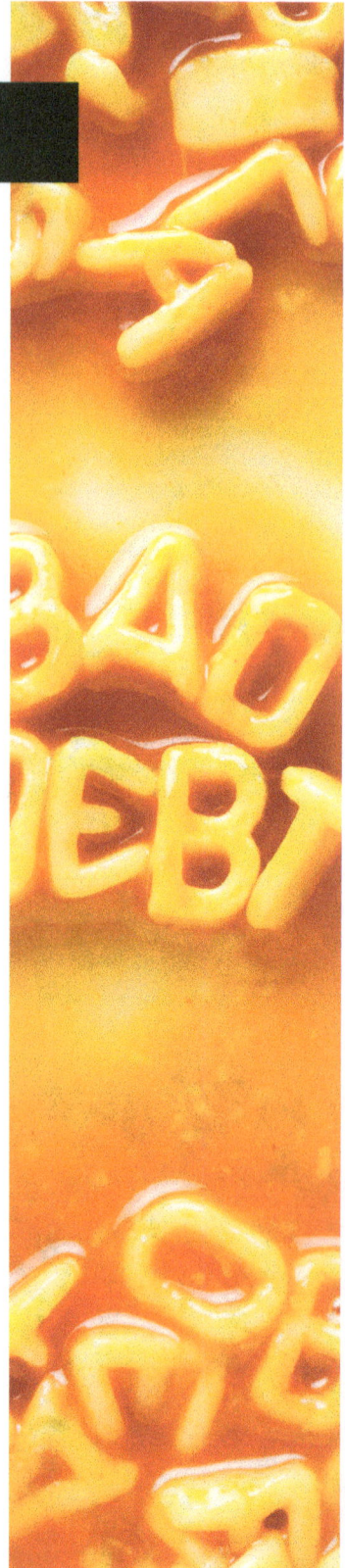

29.

"AGING SCHEDULES"

Aging Schedules generally come in two forms: Accounts Receivable aging and Accounts Payable aging. Quite simply they are a tracking of how long a receivable or a payable has existed on the books and not been addressed, ie., paid to us or by us.

For example: with Accounts Receivable we track how long it's been since each receivable existed, and not paid. The Aging Schedule generally tracks Account Receivable into 30-day groups. In Business we do this to understand how much of our Receivables are a little late, very late, or extremely late.

Accounts Payable Aging schedules do the same thing, but remember this is a measurement of bills we need to pay that we are late on paying.

30.

"DEBITS AND CREDITS"

The basic elements or entries in common accounting are Debits and Credits, and they are essential to understanding any accounting system. However, understanding them can be a little tricky.

It is important to note than Debits generally increase totals, but can increase both good and bad things like assets (good) and expenses (bad) for accounting purposes. Likewise, Credits can also affect good and bad things such as Revenue and Liabilities. It's important to understand their importance and two-sided nature to analyze bank statements and other financial statements. But be careful to understand the manners, both negative and positive, in which both can be used.

reliable control
expense statement asset revenue
register posting auditing debit
balance collecting loss
cash
accounting bookkeeping income accountancy
management
structured information
credit financial reporting sheet
ledger recording business transaction
petty decision account

31.

"GENERALLY ACCEPTED ACCOUNTING PRINCIPLES (GAAP)"

The basic accounting system used all over the world is known as the Double Entry Accounting system and it was reportedly created by monks in the 14th century. To ensure that all people who use the system use it in similar fashion, accounting industries have created a set of commonly understood rules and practices known as Generally Accepted Accounting Principles, usually known by the acronym GAAP.

In financial reporting for public companies, the principles of GAAP accounting govern how companies account and report the financial results.

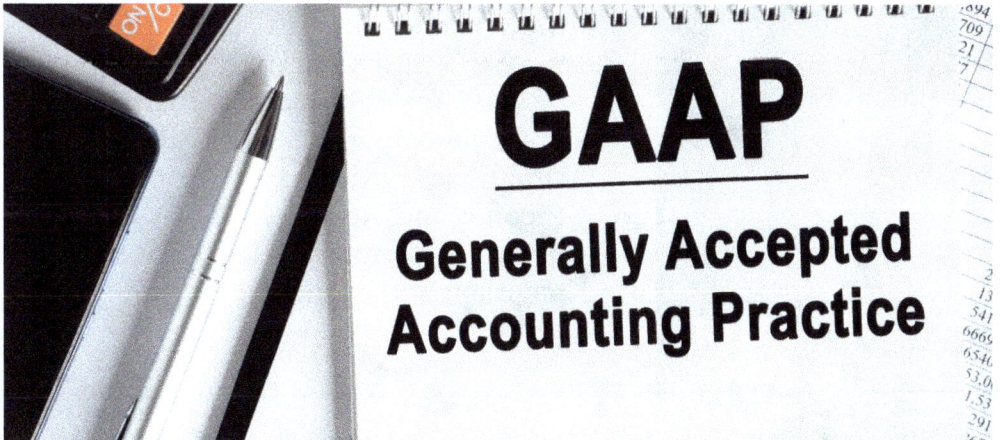

GAAP

Generally Accepted Accounting Practice

32.

"ACCRUED INTEREST / REVENUE / INCOME"

In the accrual system of accounting, certain numbers are generated when an event has occurred, not when the cash is received. An example: revenue exists when a sale is made, not when the payment for a sale is received. So things can accrue before the monies have been paid.

Accrued Interest happens when holding bonds even though the payment only happens on lets say, a semi-annual basis. The holder of the bond is entitled to the accrued interest as long as they possess the bond. If they were to sell the bond, they would be paid for the Accrued Interest until the date it was sold. Similar situations exist for Accrued Income and Revenue. Values are being generated despite no payment at that specific time.

33.

"RECONCILE / BANK RECONCILIATION"

An important activity that every small business should complete on a monthly basis is the reconciling of what was put into their accounting system reconciled against the bank statement they received for their accounts. Errors happen, and they happen on both sides of this equation. This important process will catch errors that can affect both your cash flow and financial results.

The process is simple: Verify that all the entries on your bank statement match all the entries in your business accounting system. Additionally, it helps greatly that someone with intimate knowledge of the business and its spending is doing the Reconciliation to assure that only legitimate entries have hit the bank statement.

34.

"THE ACCOUNTING EQUATION"

The basic formulation that undergirds all of the Double Entry Accounting system is known as The Accounting Equation and it is as follows:

Assets - Liabilities = Owner's Equity

It is sometimes shuffled around to where Assets are alone on one side of the equation, but that is the same thing just reformulated. It can be adjusted even further to have Liabilities be the summation. Irrespective The Accounting Equation always says the same thing. Essentially, what we have minus what we owe is what we are worth.

Assets - Liabilities = Equity

35.

"COMPLIANCE"

Somewhat of a broad term with different elements in different parts of the business, Compliance is the assuring that the activities and policies of a company comply with rules and regulations. In Business, there are legal Compliance issues, but also there can be regulatory Compliance issues pertaining to how a company acts in its business.

Compliance should not be taken lightly as running a foul of regulations and laws can lead to substantial financial pain and even bankruptcy of a company. Many companies will have a compliance department or a compliance officer but oftentimes for small business it is a all hands-on deck approach to managing things.

36.

"RETAINED EARNINGS"

Generally one of the more complicated of the accounting elements registered on financial statements, Retained Earnings is confusing as people often think of it as a pile of cash given its name, when in fact, it is more of an accounting construct. It represents the amount of profits leftover for business purposes.

Retained Earnings are those earnings that a company produces, but does not divest to shareholders. It is a figure that grows year after year if the company is profitable, or conversely decreases if the company is not. Again Retained Earnings do not represent a large sum of cash to be deployed or divested, it is an accumulation of profits not divested over time, hence retained.

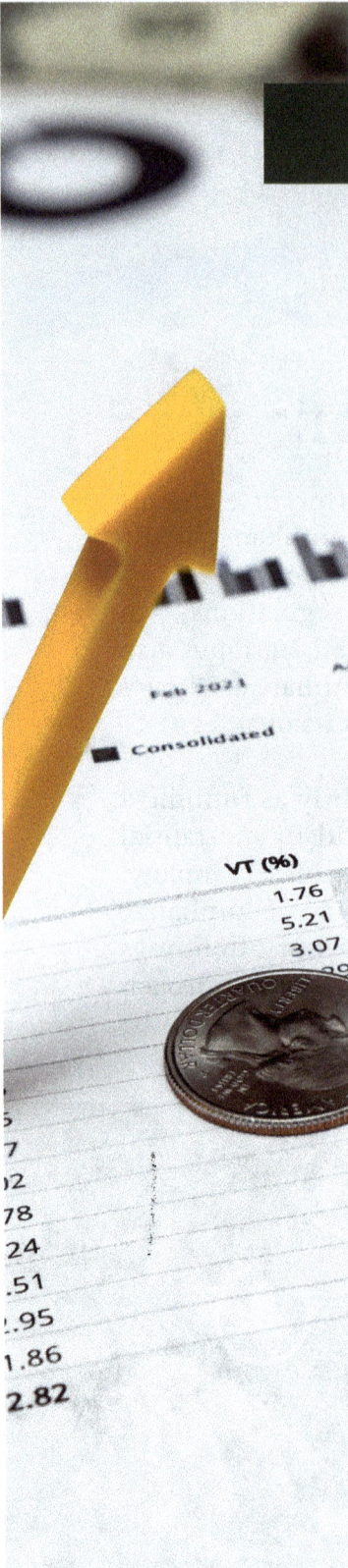

37.

"SALES TAX / VALUE ADDED TAX"

In most but not all jurisdictions (city, state, & federal), there is a tax placed on End sales made within that jurisdiction. These Sales Taxes are paid by the customer buying a finished product. The company must capture the Sales Tax for future submission to the appropriate tax authority.

It is essential that small businesses collect the Sales Tax, account for them on their books, and ultimately submit the tax (cash) to the jurisdiction. Failure to do so is tax fraud, and can result in huge penalties and even jail time.

Certain countries use a Value Added Tax, which taxes product sales each step of the way in production versus just taxing one time at the sale of the end product.

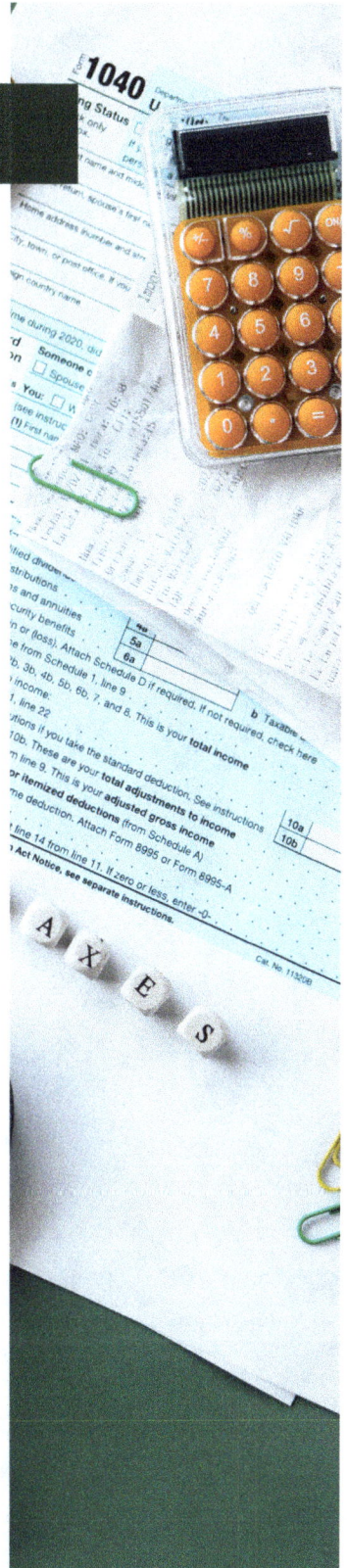

MARKETING, STRATEGY & MANAGEMENT

BUSINESS BASICS EXPLAINED SIMPLY

MARKETING

BUSINESS BASICS EXPLAINED SIMPLY

1.

"MARKETING"

A broad definition of Marketing is all activities that a business undertakes to have its current and potential customer bases exhibit a certain behavior. Sometimes that behavior is an action, like moving a client to buy our product. Other times, it's a behavior like a customer feeling certain ways about our company (trustworthy, high quality etc.).

Altogether, Marketing is about taking actions to affect behaviors, and sales, in terms of a sales team or Salesforce, is a subset area of Marketing, usually the most important element under the rubric. Advertising, promotion, and public relations are also subsets underneath the broad definition of Marketing.

2.

"TARGETING"

Targeting in business is the act of using the tools of Marketing to reach a specifically-defined group of people or businesses. Targeting consists of both essential efforts, first defining the audience for the Marketing tools, and then using those tools to reach them with the appropriate product, message, and price.

Developing targets consists of an analysis of the audience, interests, trends, and preferences and figuring out how they correspond to the product or service a company is planning to offer them. Thereafter, a Marketing campaign is designed specifically and directly for this well-defined group.

3.

"CROSS-CHANNEL MARKETING"

As the name implies, Cross-Channel Marketing is the process of producing a Marketing campaign across different marketing platforms or 'channels' to increase its reach, efficiency and results. Channels in this definition can be quite various and include emails, print advertising, radio, television ads, social media etc. In fact any avenue in which a company can reach out to its customer base is consider a marketing channel.

An example of Cross-Channel Marketing would be when a company does a special offer on its products and promotes the offer in an email, on its website in social media posts, and various advertising campaigns.

4.

"DIGITAL MARKETING"

Digital Marketing, broadly defined, is the tools in marketing that a company uses that are communicated through digital means. It includes mail communication and online ads. Essentially anything delivered via the Internet can fit under the rubric Digital Marketing.

Digital Marketing has become perhaps the most important tool for company marketers. The main reason for this is the incredible cost reductions from past ways of marketing such as Television, Radio and Print advertising. The reduced costs of Digital Marketing allow companies to achieve better returns on their Marketing dollars, and often better relationships with the potential and existing customer base.

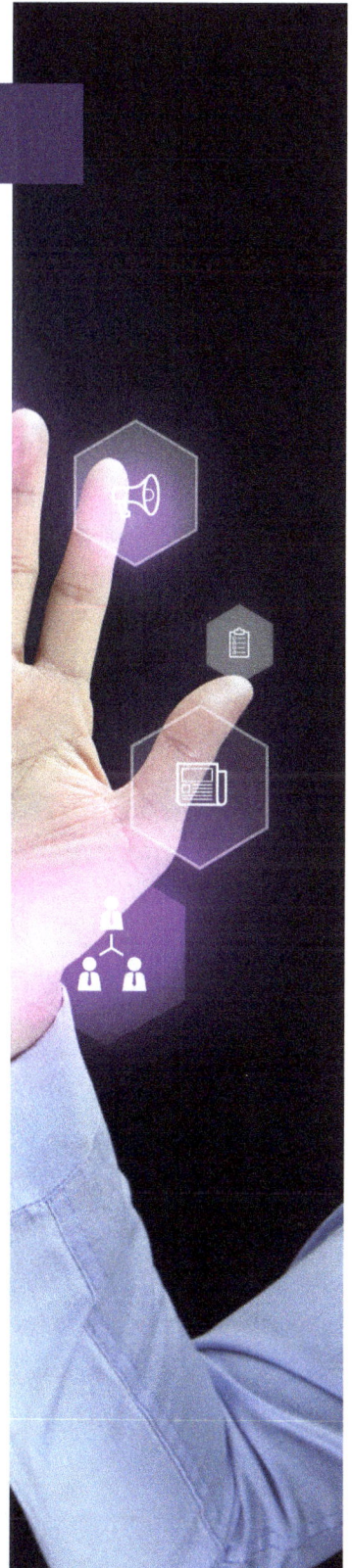

5.

"INFLUENCER MARKETING"

Influencer Marketing is using a person with a sufficiently large social media following to promote either your company or its products to an audience, their followers. Essentially a deal is made between the Influencer and the company to compensate the Influencer for their promotion of something.

Examples, on a largest scale, is Kim Kardashian, who earns an incredible rate for promoting products on the Internet and in person at events. This is driven by the staggering size of her following. But there are options for Small Businesses to engage smaller, more targeted and more affordable influencers. If targeted well, meaning the influencer has a following similar to the product hoping to be promoted, Influencer Marketing can be cost effective.

6.

"POINT-OF-SALE (POS) MARKETING"

Point-of-Sale Marketing is those elements and efforts utilized to sell or inform customers at the Point-of-Sale, meaning the cash register. This can be in the store, at public events or even often at a professional industry conference. Basically, wherever companies are interacting in-person with their customer base.

P.O.S. Marketing often includes signs, brochures and pamphlets. Even salespeople at a conference and can be a very effective tool for getting pertinent information to your potential customers, specifically at an opportune moment: the moment of sale.

Studies show that good POS marketing can increase both the average sale and total sales for Business if implemented well.

145

7.

"UNITY OF MESSAGE"

Unity of Message speaks to the imperative of marketers to design all the elements in their marketing, from the product design to the messaging to their pricing to their ad placement choices to speak with one united voice and be designed with unity throughout these various elements.

The understanding here is to ensure that the desired placement on the Price Quality graph of your products and company are all in unison with the messaging the company is projecting to the public or target market. Specifically that lower quality products are associated with lower pricing, quality and messaging, and vice versa, in that higher quality products are matched with appropriate pricing, promotion and placement.

8.

"BRAND ASSOCIATION"

Brand Association is when a target market associates certain qualitative characteristics with a brand. Hopefully they are good ones, such as quality, value and style with Rolex. Sometimes the public feels it's "cool" to wear certain clothes or drive certain cars and this is a result of the Marketing creating strong associations with their products. But often bad associations can be created and they can have a substantial negative effect on sales. Think Kmart.

Generally, as marketers, we are trying to build strong Brand Associations as they tend to lead to brand loyalty, which leads ultimately to increased sales over time.

BRANDING

9.

"THE FOUR PS OF MARKETING"

Price.
Product.
Placement.
Promotion.

These are the levers of Marketing at every business's disposal. There are more complicated schemes to describe the elements of Marketing, but I find this one simple and thorough enough for Small Businesses. Four simple elements you can adjust, change, overhaul, or just leave as they are.

The Price you charge. The Product you design. Your Placement on the Price-Quality matrix. And lastly, your Promotion in the world.

10.

"SEARCH ENGINE OPTIMIZATION (SEO)"

Search Engine Optimization (SEO) is the process of designing websites and advertisements that are constructed to achieve better results in ranking with Search Engines such as Google and Microsoft's Bing.

The detailed process, which often adjusts without much warning, is at its core about finding key words and content that Search Engines believe will be most useful to a target audience. Then this content is placed on websites in highly-visible areas to ensure viewers who go to the site from a search or ad will be appropriately satisfied.

The goal of SEO is get higher rankings in search for key words and content, leading to more visitors to a website.

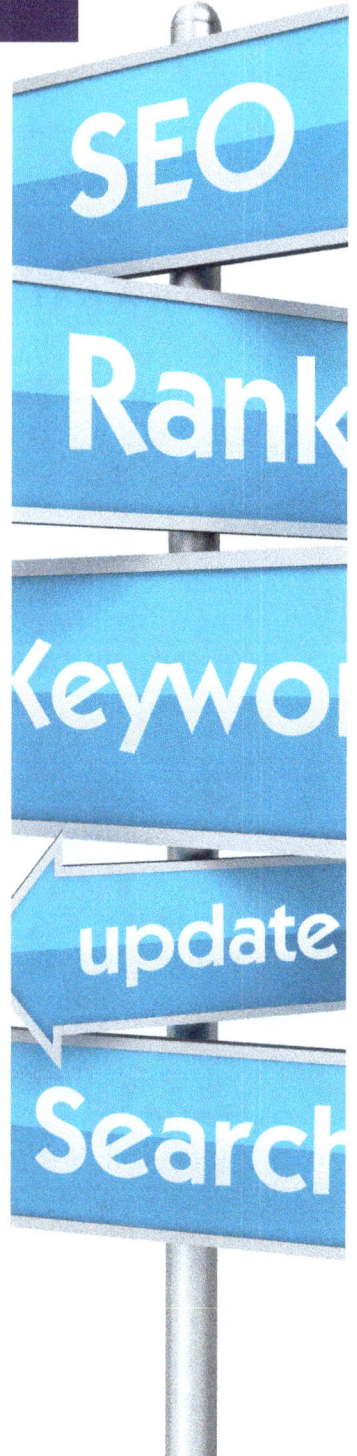

11.

"BRAND EQUITY"

In Finance, Equity is a term that means ownership value, like companies have Equity and shares on a stock exchange are also called Equity. The Marketing usage of the term varies slightly, but still implies 'owned value' in a sense.

We speak of Brand Equity to describe the inherent value of a brand in the marketplace. It is a sense of how much the public admires and respects a brand, but also how loyal and consistent the public is in terms of purchase history and future to the brand.

Some of the brands with the greatest Brand Equity are Apple, Coke, and Marlboro. As you can imagine, people who use these brands are very loyal to them in their feelings and purchases.

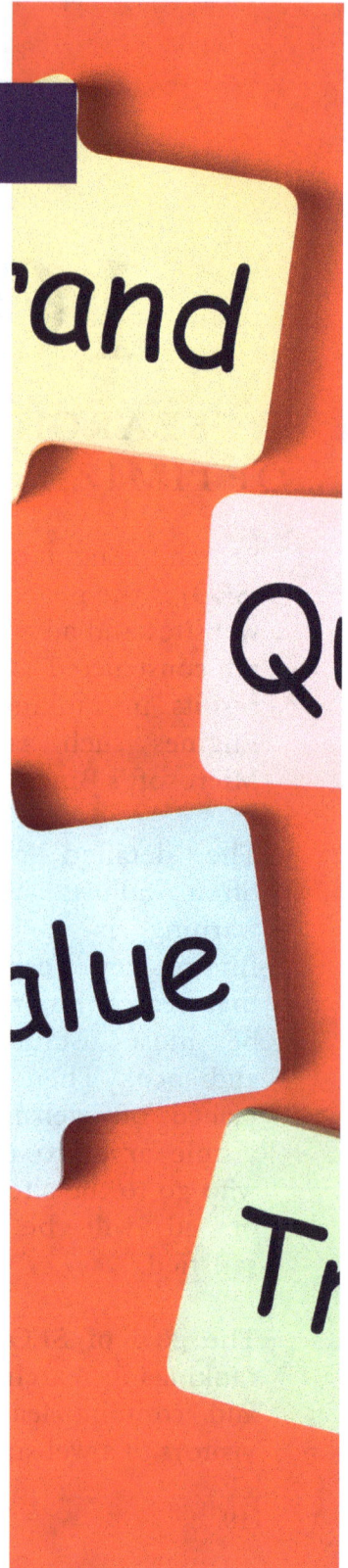

12.

"TARGET MARKET"

A Target Market is an audience or grouping that a company has decided to sell to, that the company has defined through analysis in certain specific terms. Generally Target Markets are defined by detailed demographic information such as age, income level, education, and geography.

An example: A company has a new sneaker built for older people. So they are 'targeting' the product at an age group of over 60, perhaps with an income over $80,000 and who live primarily in the Northern states who are college educated etc.

Often there are several different Target Markets that companies are designing products for with each Target Market having different defining demographic parameters.

le

Me

Requirements for Profitable Segments

ial

Ac

13.

"MARKET SEGMENTATION

After defining a target market for a product, companies will break down that market into different market segments, which is aptly named, Market Segmentation.

This is essentially dividing the target market further, usually through more specifically defined demographic and geographic determinants so that more precise marketing can occur.

To follow on a sneaker example, a Market Segment might be those in the target market who share particular interests like jogging or those who wear certain types of sneakers for a specific health reason. Each is a segment within a large target market.

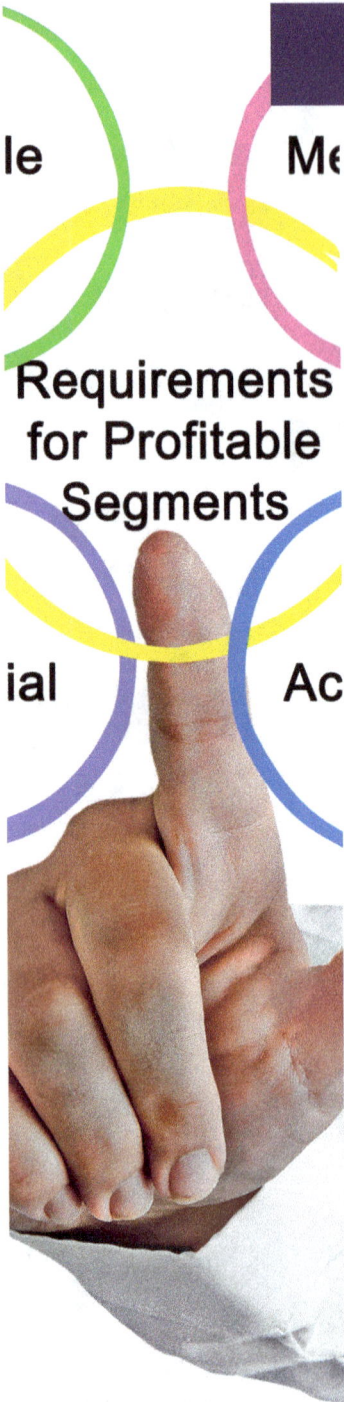

14.

"CUSTOMER PROFILES"

After researching and deciding on your target markets and the market segments underneath that, often businesses will create Customer Profiles that are detailed summaries of the characteristics that represent people in their market segments. Because in business with Marketing, the better we know the people we are selling to, the better we will be at developing Marketing campaigns that are successful with them.

Thus Customer Profiles are created to drill down further with more research and more clear definitions of the customer, their interests, and the drivers that are facilitating their buying decisions.

15.

"MARKETING MIX"

Marketing Mix speaks to the offering of elements a company uses to promote its products. Marketing elements include traditional advertising elements such as print, radio and television ads as well as social media advertising and promotion. It can also include event and influencer marketing. Essentially any element of a Marketing plan is the Marketing Mix.

Oftentimes we calculate the Marketing Mix in terms of dollars spent as a percentage of the total spent. For example, if a company spends $50,000 in total marketing dollars, and of that total it spends $5,000 in print ads, it spends 10% in print.

It is strongly recommended to have a diversified Marketing Mix, with monies spent on multiple various elements.

16.

"TOTAL ADDRESSABLE MARKET (TAM)"

The Total Addressable Market is a marketing metric which attempts to capture the total size that exists for a company to sell their product to. It is in essence everyone who might purchase a product or service.

Companies use the TAM estimate to show investors that their product or company has sufficient and even ample potential in the marketplace because the total possible buyers, the TAM, is sufficiently large.

Often TAMs are absurdly large estimates, and also often they are not the most believable or relevant metrics.

17.

"CONVERSION RATE"

Conversation Rate is defined simply as the percentage of some metric divided by the number of confirmed sales. This can be applied to various elements in Marketing such as sales presentations per sale or advertisements viewed per sale. It is a measure of how well that element is leading to the most important metric: Sales.

This calculation is especially important when considering social media ads. Many companies are particularly interested in the rate of Sales that come from either site visits in total or clicks.

Again, the calculation is clear. If a company closes 1 sale for every 100 people who visit their site, the conversion rate, the rate of sales to visitors is 1%.

LEADS

PROSPE

CUSTO

18.

"VALUE PROPOSITION"

In Business, more specifically in the Marketing of a business, product or service, the phrase Value Proposition is used to describe the unique elements that a company or a product uses to make itself attractive and sell itself to its target customer. Often shortened into the lingo Value Prop, it's the specific values in the product that is pitched in the marketing.

What is the Value Proposition of an iPhone ? The iPhone delivers an incredible quality product, and a first-tier camera, incredible styling, millions of apps, etc. That list details the valuable elements and aspects of an iPhone that make it attractive to potential customers.

19.

"LOYALTY PROGRAMS"

Loyalty Programs, simply, are Marketing programs that are designed to generate loyalty in the customer base. From the most basic to the most complex, all forms of Loyalty Programs seek to generate both qualitative and quantitative results. They can take countless shapes and sizes.

Common examples are subscription programs that give added benefits with repeated sales. Or maybe a running discount program where the fifth purchase is free. Or money back over time when certain sales thresholds are met.

Small Businesses can develop different Loyalty Programs that lock in customers and incentivize them to increase their purchases over time.

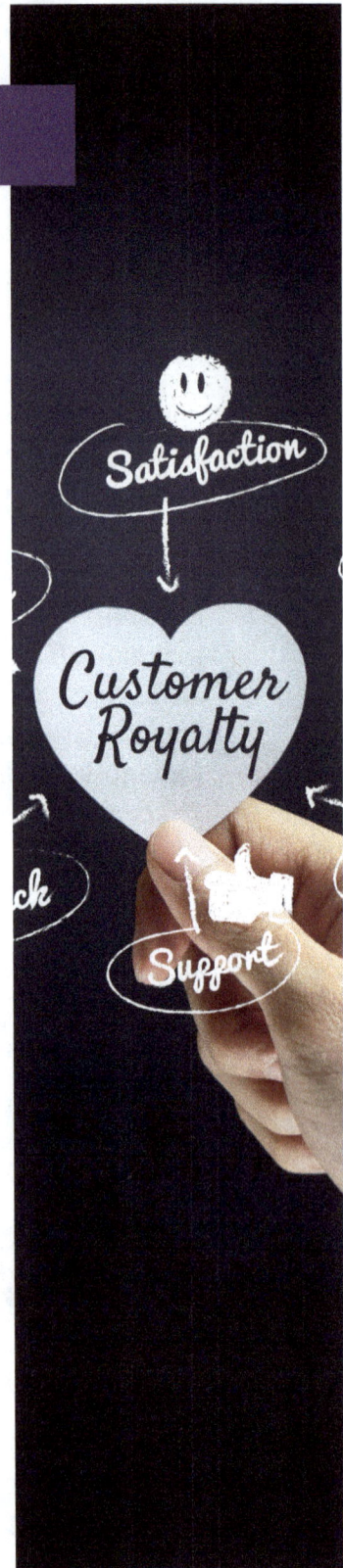

20.

"DRIVERS OF BUYING DECISIONS"

This phrase is also referred to using Purchasing Decisions, but the Drivers of Buying Decisions are those specific detailed elements that incite a target buyer to finally and fully put down the credit card or money and buy the product or service. A goal of all marketers is finding out those specific elements, those Drivers of Buying Decisions, and then using them in Marketing communications.

For many products and target markets, the drivers are similar, and include price, product quality, brand associations, etc. Often the Primary Driver is a combination of these factors, and a knowledge of the intensity of each element in driving a customers buying decision is invaluable.

21.

"MARKET RESEARCH"

Broadly defined, Market Research is all efforts made by a company to better understand both its current and potential customer base. There are many varied approaches to Market Research, but some the most commonly used tools are surveys, questionnaires, focus groups, and perhaps most effective, in-person interviews.

The benefits of doing Market Research are found in both the cost reduction in marketing expenditures through better informed decisions as well as the increased sales that result. Knowing the likes, dislikes, preferences, drivers of buying decisions, etc. is invaluable to companies as they build product designs, construct marketing messages and pricing schemes.

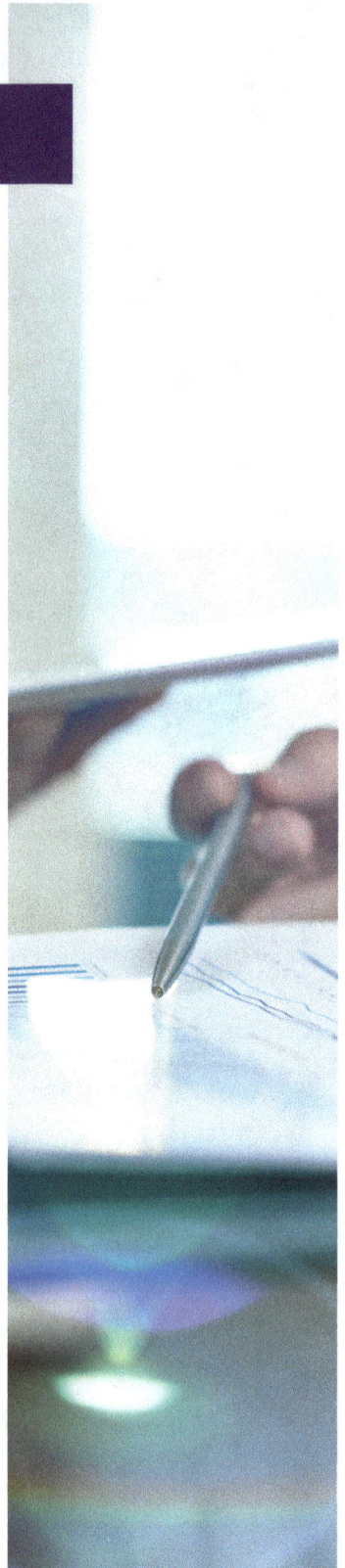

22.

"REBRANDING"

There comes the time in every product or company's life cycle when it is necessary to refresh the Marketing, thereby adjusting, or more largely, changing the look, feel and messaging surrounding the product or company. We call this refresh, or overhaul as the case may be, a Rebranding.

Perhaps the product's messaging has gotten stale or the target market's interests have moved away from where the product is placed (think: cigarettes to e-cigs). Perhaps the company's goals and objectives have changed over time through acquisition and product changes (think Facebook becoming Meta). A rebranding is reintroducing the product or company to its customer base and hopefully new users through changes in various elements of its marketing: logos, colors, taglines.

23.

"REMARKETING CAMPAIGN"

Tied to social media advertising, Remarketing campaigns are advertising campaigns driven by computer algorithms that repeatedly show the same or similar ads to someone who has expressed interest in a product or company, by virtue of the person clicking on a social media ad.

Remarketing, as in marketing again, is a very valuable tool to increase sales as most customers do not purchase a product based on a one-time viewing of an ad. Social Media company technology allows their platforms to repeatedly show ads to people who express interest, thereby affording the viewer more chances for additional interactions. Studies show that Remarketing campaigns are very effective in driving sales.

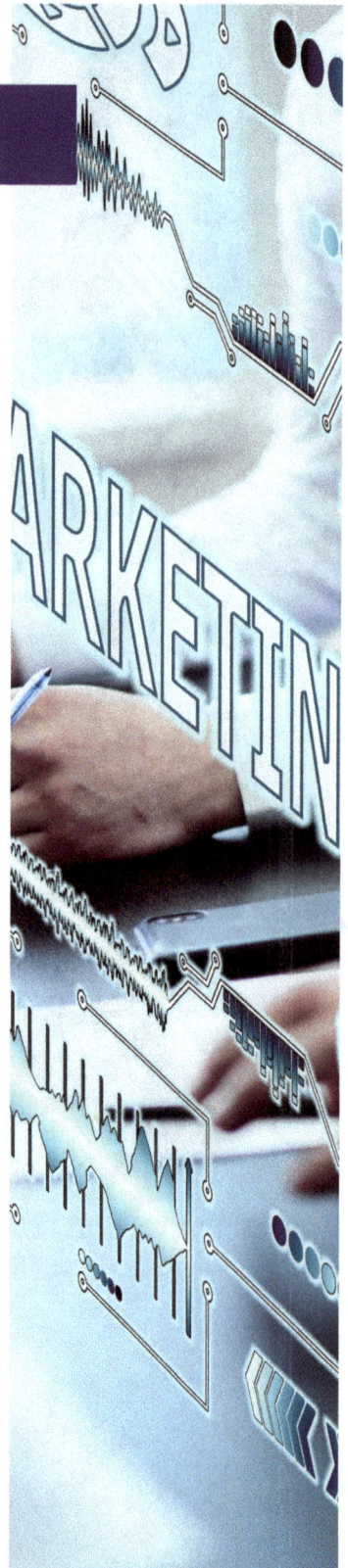

24.

"TOP-OF-MIND AWARENESS"

Top-of-Mind Awareness (sometimes written by its acronym, TOMA) is the concept that brands wish to remain the first choice thought of in a category of products and brands. To remain Top of Mind is to be the first thing that comes to mind for a customer when a particular niche is recalled in memory. For example, someone saying Kellogg's when asked to think of the name a breakfast cereal brand.

As one can imagine, there is great sales power in achieving TOMA status, especially with buyers in competitive industries where there are countless choices available to a buying public. Being the first brand or product thought of often evidences a level of establishment and advantage, something all want.

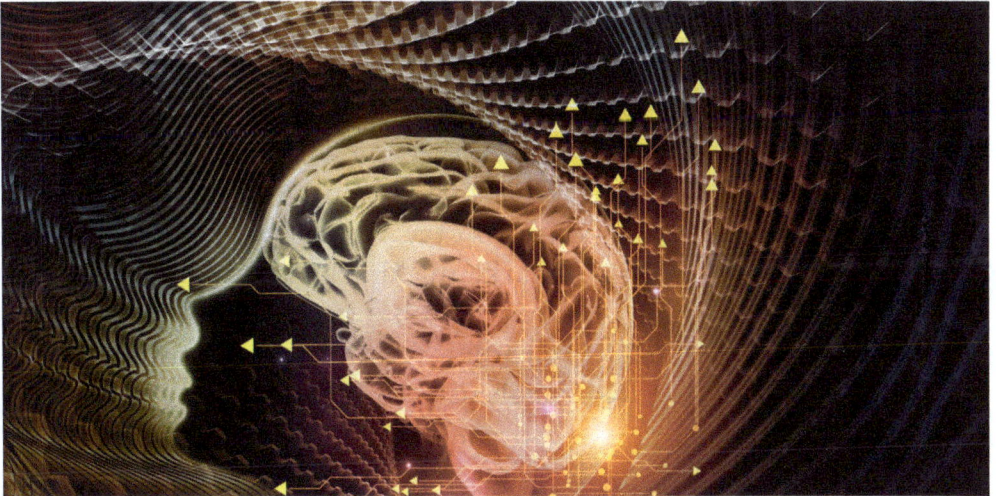

25.

"R.O.A.S."
RETURN ON ADVERTISING SPEND

Return On Advertising Spend, often abbreviated by its acronym, R.O.A.S., is an important metric that many marketers use to understand whether they are getting a sufficient return on investment of their marketing dollars. It is a simple calculation, I hope, dividing total advertising spend by the sounds directly achieved by that advertising spend.

Most small businesses should be shooting for an R.O.A.S of greater than 3 to 1, meaning that for each dollar in advertising spending they are generating $1 in total sales directly related to that advertising spend. Often the key is to try to eliminate other marketing dollars spending from the analysis in order to get a clearer return on investment analysis.

26.

"DEMOGRAPHIC ANALYSIS"

Demographic Analysis is the dividing of target markets into different categories separated by specific characteristics, either physical or social grouping. The main examples are age, sex, race, and geography, but can also include non-physical breakdowns such belief systems and interests.

Marketing departments use Demographic Analysis to better define the specific target markets interested in the product or service the company sells. The belief is the better you can define your target market through Demographic Analysis, the better you can develop messages that speak to those specific markets based on their demographics.

27.

"MERCHANDISING"

An essential concept in retail stores, whether brick-and-mortar or online stores, Merchandising concerns the display of goods within a location as well as any offers and deals related to merchandise displayed in that location.

Countless studies have shown that how merchandise is laid out in a store, or even in a certain section of a store, can have a dramatic effect on customer buying patterns and overall sales. Merchandising can consist of location design as well as product grouping and even include tying promotions to the layout of goods in a retail environment.

All retail operations should consider thoroughly how goods are displayed in order to effectuate the greatest results.

28.

"CALL TO ACTION"

A Call to Action, (often denoted by the acronym CTA), is the wording in ads and websites that remind, instruct, and even cajole a viewer to take an action desired by the company. The most famous Call-to-Action of all-time is the classic Buy Now! But they do come in many shapes and sizes such as Learn More, Enroll Here, Contact Us and on and on.

The key of course, is the verb which instructs a viewer to take some defined action. Studies show repeatedly that simply instructing viewers to take some action with a CTA substantially increases viewer engagement over the lack of a CTA. Thus it is crucial that in both online and older media communications (newspaper ads, billboards, radio, television) that a clear, noticeable and simple Call-to-Action is well presented.

29.

"MARKETING COPY / COLLATERAL"

The writing that makes up the basis of a piece of Marketing is broadly called the Copy. It can be in many places including the language used in ads or on websites, even instructions, pamphlets and brochures. In essence, all writing on Marketing pieces is considered Marketing Copy written by copywriters.

Marketing Collateral is a broad term used to define all items that are produced by a company to market to their audiences. Again, it is a term used to cover anything from brand websites to salesman brochures to advertisements, both digital and analog.

30.

"DISPOSABLE INCOME"

So many businesses sell products that are not essentials for daily living such as food, gas and electricity, medicine, but are products that fall into the "want-to-have" categories. In Business, these products are bought with what is known as Disposable Income, their usable cash, leftover after a consumer purchases their essentials.

It is essential when marketing your company's products to have an understanding as to which category your products fall into, Consumer Essentials or Disposable Income, and design your marketing programs according to their category as so often the recognition of this will drive messaging to the consumer.

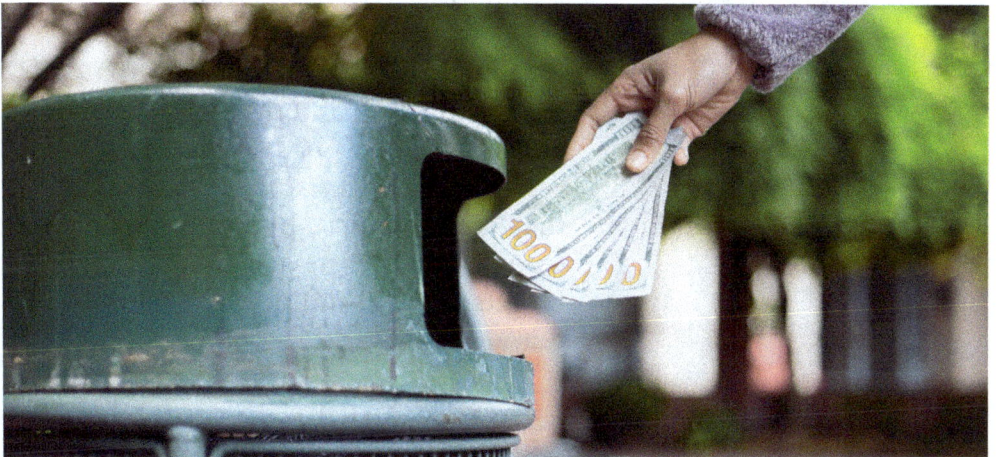

31.

"PUSH & PULL MARKETING

Push and Pull marketing are two different approaches that companies use to achieve sales objectives. Each methodology is generally used in in conjunction or simultaneously.

One of the best devices for understanding each is the comparison of Google versus Facebook ads. In Google ads, people are searching for something, they put words into the search bar and Pull advertisements to them. With the Facebook / Instagram ads approach, advertisements are pushed towards audiences that have shown an interest in certain areas. However they have requested information, or the ads that come with it, like they do in Google. One device is pulling targets to you, and one is pushing marketing at targets.

.

32.

"INBOUND / OUTBOUND MARKETING

Very similar definitionally to the Push Pull Marketing differential, Inbound and Outbound marketing approaches are differently directed efforts to achieve communication with targeted audiences. Inbound Marketing efforts are those that try to drive sales through things that incite target audiences to initiate contact with a company such as developing special content, like YouTube videos or blogs, etc.

Outbound Marketing efforts are those activities that are undertaken to drive targeted communication through pushed efforts such direct mail campaigns, commercial, advertising, direct selling with salespeople.

33.

"B2B / B2C / B2G"

These acronyms stand for the sales target a company is selling to as it's primary target.

B2B = Business to Business. That is selling to other businesses like corporate software sales, tax services.

B2C = Business to Consumer. Here are companies whose targets are individual customers, anything from restaurants to video games, and everything in between.

B2G = Business to Government. Those companies whose clients are mainly gouvernements, be they small cities or the federal government, even divisions of the US government such as The Department of Defense or Education.

34.

"ONBOARDING"

Onboarding, in a Marketing sense, is the process of bringing in or "on" new customers to your company's products or services. Similarly, Onboarding can also mean the addition of new employees or providers, which similarly are brought into the system a company uses for adding new participants.

Onboarding is of growing importance these days as web-based activities and businesses proliferate. Having new customers set up accounts, detail their preferences and personal information are essential Onboarding activities that affect how new customers react with a company initially and in the future.

35.

"ACCOUNT-BASED MARKETING (ABM)"

Account-Based Marketing, which goes by the acronym ABM, is when a company's marketing activities are designed around large targeted accounts as opposed to smaller increments such as the broad-based general public or smaller private company.

As one can imagine Account-Based Marketing depends on the industry one is in, and the size of companies that the industry contains. For example if one works in the Military, or Governmental aerodynamic industry, given the size and relatively small number of potential customers, designing marketing efforts strategically in an ABM format is more appropriate and more effective.

36.

"FRICTION / PAIN POINTS"

Friction or Pain Points is the name marketers give to those elements and aspects in a sales process that are inhibiting final sales from occuring. Friction / Pain Points, specifically as the names imply, are impediments in the purchasing process that is causing customers not to complete sales. This can be a website, a product design, or even a communication issue that inhibits sales.

These words, additionally, are a way that marketers use to describe elements and aspects in a customer's status that a company's products or services are hoping to alleviate. A consumer's Friction or Pain Point represents an opportunity for alleviation with the sale of a company's product to the buyer.

37.

"RETENTION STRATEGIES"

Simply put, successful business relies on the successful Retention of current customers almost as much as it does the acquisition of new customers. Retention Strategies are activities that businesses take to ensure that current customers are retained, kept as future customers and targets for future sales efforts. Retention Strategies can also be focused internally on company employees.

Classic marketing Retention Strategies include special discounts and promotions for loyalty club members, first-look or private introduction promotions and personalized tiers of service based on loyalty or business volume.

38.

"WORD-OF-MOUTH MARKETING (WOMM)"

A little known fact is that Word-of-Mouth Marketing is that most effective and cost efficient way for companies to produce a following and sales. Simply put, Word-of-Mouth Marketing is when some client recommends a product or service of one company to another person. A broader definition can also include online recommendations and reviews, though the proximity of the two people (friends, family, colleagues) has a much stronger effect.

Studies by Nielsen show that 92% of consumers trust recommendations from connections more than other forms of Marketing, and other studies show the incredible power of WOM marketing in final buying decisions. There are strategies to emphasize WOM.

39.

"MARKETING AUTOMATION"

An essential tool for successful Marketing especially for small businesses that don't have large budgets or large teams, Marketing Automation is, as expected, the process of certain important Marketing activities occurring automatically without the constant effort or supervision of a person.

There are countless examples of Marketing Automation when broadly defined, and some do take significant time and technological investments to set up and implement. Some of the most common are automated messages after a purchase on a website and Email marketing letters triggered by a certain event such an automated welcome letter when someone joins your mailing list or an email reminder when an online cart is abandoned.

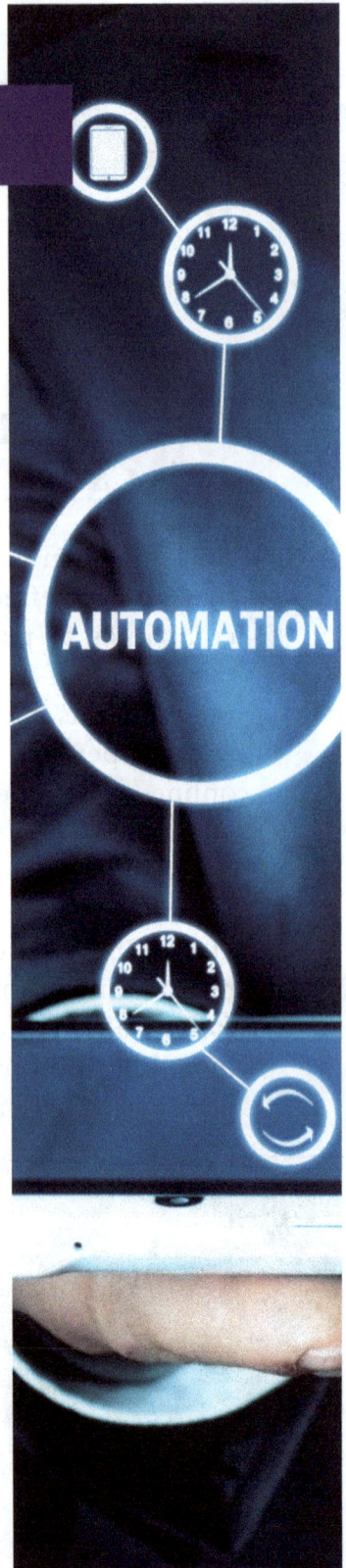

STRATEGY

BUSINESS BASICS EXPLAINED SIMPLY

1.

"THE PRICE-QUALITY MATRIX"

Traditionally in Business, there is a relationship between the price you pay for something and the quality inherent in that item. While not always true, there is a general expectation in people's minds that a price-to-quality relationship exists.

In Business, we often view this relationship in graphical form with Price on one axis, and Quality on the other. Think if you will the difference between Dollar Store and Tiffany's. One expects lower prices but lower quality at the Dollar store, and higher prices with higher quality at Tiffany's.

Where a company or product falls on the graph is oftentimes thought of as its Marketing placement.

High price, Low Quality	High price, High Quality
Low price, Low Quality	Low price, High Quality

PRICE

QUALITY

2.

"LOSS LEADER"

Loss Leader is a marketing strategy where a company sells a product at or near its costs of making the product so that the company makes very little or even no gross margin on each sale they make, but drive interest in the product or the store.

So why would a company sell a product where it makes no money? The answer is in the hope that this deal, which they will promote in stores and ads if they're smart, will bring in customers to their shop where they otherwise might not have visited. Additionally, the hope is that customers will buy this product deal but also will spend money on other products because they came to the store, and these other products bought will have a full margin associated with it.

3.

"PRICE ELASTICITY"

In economics, Elasticity of Price refers to the effect on sales of an increase or decrease in the price of a product. If a price on a product is raised and there is a material drop-off in sales, the product is said to be Price Elastic. If there is no substantial drop-off in sales with the increase, it is said to be inelastic. It's similar for decreases.

When raising the price of any product or service, one should always consider Price Elasticity. Always ask the question thinking in terms of net absolute dollars: Will the increase I am passing through generate such a drop-off in sales that the net effect on absolute dollars is detrimental? If there's a net detrimental absolute dollars, don't do the price increase.

4.

"KEY PERFORMANCE INDICATORS (KPIS)"

KPIs, the acronym for Key Performance Indicators, are statistics about the business that are measured and tracked over time, and indicate if the business is making progress on various objectives and fronts deemed important.

Examples often used are the number of Social Media followers, the amount of visitors to websites in a given month, the number of purchases made on a website in a quarter, etc. One can set-up almost endless different KPIs and it's important to tailor those you use to your specific business and industry.

But remember: Sales, Gross Margin, Cash Flow and Profitability are the ultimate KPIs.

5.

"CUSTOMER ACQUISITION COSTS"

Customer Acquisition Costs is an analysis that hopes to help one understand how much it costs to get new customers to either buy or support a business.

The essential calculation is dividing the total marketing expenditures by the total number of newly "acquired" customers in a given period. The calculation generates a cost per new customer figure which will change over time with the Marketing expenditures and effectiveness.

This analysis can be very illustrative of both the eagerness of customers for a company's products as well as how effective the marketing of the company is in being able to capture new clients.

6.

"SALES FUNNEL"

They come in many different shapes and sizes depending on the type of company and the industry, but in their essence, a Sales Funnel is a series of steps designed by a company to move a customer through the long voyage from awareness to purchase. The metaphor of the funnel is used to capture the fact that the closer we get to a final sale, the tighter the connection with the customer must be to achieve the final leap to a sale.

Typical Sales Funnel steps include achieving customer awareness (through ads), gaining customer interaction (visiting website) then getting a small customer commitment (email contact), generating further engagement (downloading free material) ultimately leading to final larger customer commitment, let's say, an actual purchase.

7.

"BCG MATRIX"

The BCG Matrix, otherwise known as the Growth Share Matrix, is a graphical marketing analysis that positions a company's products based on the cash generation of the product on one axis, and the cash investment into the product on the other axis. It was first developed at the Boston Consulting Group, hence the acronym, BCG.

This analysis is designed to help strategic thinking by trying to answer questions about which of a company's products deserve more marketing investment or less, more effort internally or perhaps review for external disposition (sale to 3rd parties, other companies).

The four quadrants of the Matrix are broken down into Stars, Cash Cows, Unsures and Dogs based Cash Generation and Cash Usage.

8.

"LANDING PAGE"

A Landing Page is a page setup on your website that is designed to offer or deliver something special and specific to a visitor to that page alone. It is not the Home Page, though very often, the Home Page is where most visitors land on your site.

Most often, a Landing page is set-up for visitors to receive a special offer. This page will have a unique link that is placed in some form of customer communication like a social media post or an email blast. The reader clicks the link and is taken to this Landing Page on the website, which cannot be found on the website's normal menu.

9.

"A/B TESTING"

As stressed before elsewhere, great messaging is essential for the success of any marketing campaign. So how do we know if the messaging we're using to our target audience is the best or even good? We do A/B testing of the message and the ads.

A/B testing is essential doing different marketing pieces and ads with different messages to see which ad or marketing piece generates the best results. It is not limited to two.

If one ad with a certain message is generating a better response, however that is defined, logic dictates that we target our investment spending on that message as compared with the others. Thus we are using AB testing to refine and hopefully perfect our messaging in real world circumstances.

10.

"LIFE CYCLES"

Both products and companies have what is known as Life Cycles, that is, they typically have periods of idea gestation, research and development, growth, slowing growth and stagnation then finally obsolescence. Of course, with both products and companies, sometimes a change in a product or a refreshing of offerings to the public from a company can reset where a company or product is in its lifecycle.

Understanding a company's location on its lifecycle can be useful as a strategic analysis that helps companies to understand whether different levels of investment are warranted or whether more muted spending is the appropriate course of action.

11.

"CREATING URGENCY"

In Business, the idea of Creating Urgency, in essence "purchasing" urgency in the minds of potential buyers, has been a hallmark of Marketing since its beginning. Every "Buy Now" and "Get It While It Lasts" and "Limited Time Offer" is trying to Create Urgency.

The goal of Creating Urgency is to inspire in a potential buyer the need to act quickly on something, like a Special Offer. Historically it does work on a consumer base, driving increased, timely sales if the product is appreciated by its target market. Creating Urgency is a goal for all Marketing programs.

12.

"EMAIL BLASTS"

An Email Blast is a Marketing tool whereby a company sends a well-designed email to a hopefully large database of contacts it has generated over time. The goal here is to communicate with this database of contacts to inform them of something useful, important or valuable to the audience.

There are several companies like MailChimp and Constant Contact that offers services that help businesses. In fact, each of these companies actually offers a free level of service, which companies can use very effectively.

Email Blasts are an extremely cost-effective tool to reach a target audience and should be a part of any business's, large or small, Marketing arsenal.

13.

"SEASONALITY"

The majority of businesses have fluctuations based on the time of the year, and sometimes even have large movements by month. In business, we call these fluctuations based on a calendar timing, Seasonality. The most famous seasonal effect is the Christmas season for retailers, but also the summer season for flip-flop sales. It effects producers and retailers alike.

While operations are continuing throughout the year, there are certain months that are more essential and active, and it's important to a business to plan for Seasonality as it effects inventory and cash. Forecasting these fluctuations in advance based on past years' experience helps one survive and capitalize.

14.

"FOOT-IN-THE-DOOR SALES APPROACH"

One of the two main approaches of selling is called the Foot-in-the-Door approach. Here someone making a sales pitch designs a proposal on a relatively small scale with the goal of getting the client or customer to purchase a beginner position. The hope in the future is that the client sees the value after the starter position is taken and that they increase their order volume over time.

This can be an extremely effective sales approach as it limits the risk that a client must take on to begin with your product or company. Hence you get your foot in the door so that in the future you can open the door wider.

15.

"DOOR-IN-THE-FACE SALES APPROACH"

Another major style of selling is known as the Door-in-the-Face approach. Here the salesperson designs a proposal that includes very large investments for the client or customer to make. The expectation is that the client will not make that level of investment so the salesperson follows up with a much smaller request that seems relatively minor compared to the initial ask.

Often times this approach works because it helps the client or customer feel comfortable that they have defended against making a large investment initially. Further it helps the client feel more comfortable with the baby steps they are taking.

194

16.

"THE K.I.S.S. APPROACH"

Rather crudely put, the K.I.S.S. Approach or the KISS method is an acronym for the words, "Keep It Simple, Stupid." In almost all aspects of Business, the KISS Approach, focusing on simple answers to complex problems oftentimes can result in real benefits to the business.

This can be true in diverse areas of the Business including Finance, Messaging, and even Product design. Complexity is often a barrier to success, whether the objective be implementation or understanding, complexity is more challenging than simplicity.

Remember though: Simplicity is one of the hardest things to achieve in life.

17.

"HORIZONTAL EXPANSION"

There are two types of Expansion in the business sphere: Vertical and Horizontal. By far, Horizontal expansion is more common.

Horizontal Expansion is when a company expands itself through an acquisition of another company in its existing competitive field. Essentially, a company is expanding by buying a competitor thereby growing its revenue and size in a marketplace.

It is very common in many industries for Horizontal Expansion to occur. However, at some point, too much expansion through acquisition can reduce competition substantially, and at that point the Ferderal Government may act to block an acquisition as the reduction in competition is deemed harmful to the public.

18.

"VERTICAL EXPANSION"

There are two types of Expansion in the business sphere: Vertical and Horizontal. Vertical Expansion is an internal expansion and does not directly affect another company.

Vertical Expansion is when a company expands its control over an element in a production process, in fact normally adding a new element they control in the production process. An example is when a company who makes cars also begins to make parts that go into those cars such as tires or windshields. It is said then the company has expanded vertically.

Companies do this most often to reduce their costs assuming they can make things cheaper than the cost of buying from a supplier, thereby expanding their profitability.

19.

"ECONOMIES OF SCALE"

Economies of Scale is an economic concept that deals with a manner of reducing the costs of production. Companies hope to reduce the cost of production so that they can achieve greater gross margin, and ultimately, profitability.

The idea behind an Economy of Scale is that a substantial increase in the production of a product allows a company to achieve a lower cost per individual item produced by spreading certain costs out over a greater number of products produced. This is achieved through greater efficiencies with the higher production runs. Example: It costs $1 per book to print 5,000 books, but only costs 80¢ per book to produce 10,000 books. In this case, an Economy of Scale has been achieved.

20.

"ECONOMIES OF SCOPE"

Economies of Scope is an economic concept that deals with a manner of reducing the costs of production. Companies hope to reduce the cost of production so that they can achieve greater gross margin and ultimate profitability.

The idea behind an Economy of Scope is that an expansion in the number of different products produced allows a company to achieve a lower cost per individual item produced by spreading certain costs out over a greater number of products produced. This is achieved through greater efficiencies tied to multiple different production runs. Example: It costs $1 per book to print 5,000 copies of one book, but only costs 80¢ per book to produce 5,000 copies of two different books.

21.

"DIFFERENTIATION"

An essential concept in modern business strategic thinking, Differentiation, is the process of drawing distinctions between your company or your company's products and that of your competition.

Differentiation can happen in many different aspects and elements of the competitive arena. Examples are price, delivery systems, features and attributes, and even geographic differences. There are many ways to differentiate oneself from their competition and so often, it is essential to promote this unique differentiation in your communications to your target markets. The goal of differentiation and then the communication of it is to help your targets make their buying decision in your favor.

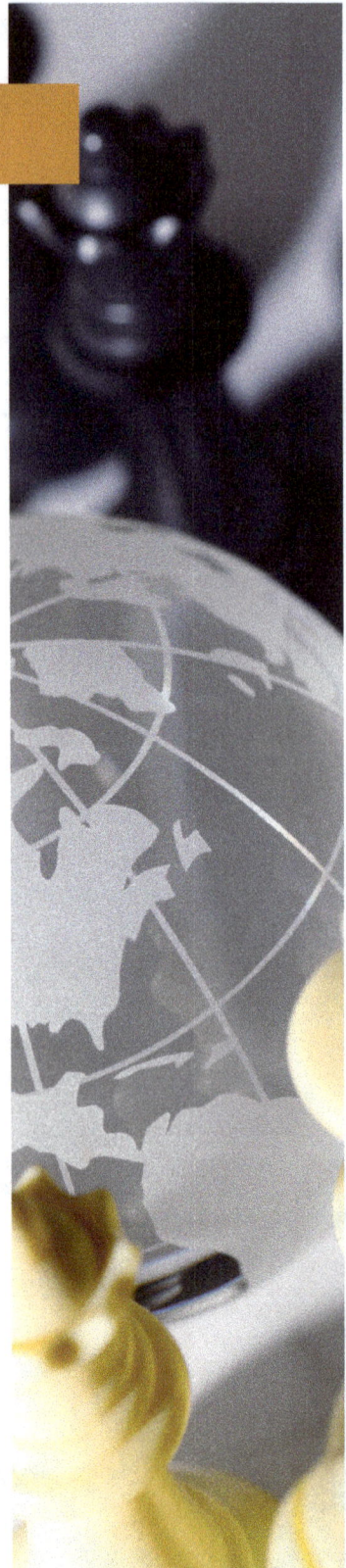

22.

"GO-TO-MARKET STRATEGY"

Go-To-Market strategy is the detailed strategic planning that is done before a company's launching of a new product. When it is done right, it is a specific blueprint that can be followed detailing each step the company intends take before the launch.

A good Go-To Market strategy planning document will contain in it elements from several, and usually all disciplines within the business including production, marketing, finance, and operations management. When done correctly, it brings together all the pertinent departments to ensure they work cohesively, in unison, to ensure the launch can be carried out successfully.

23.

"UNIQUE SELLING PROPOSITION"

Unique Selling Proposition, abbreviated to USP, is an element of the sales process where the seller highlights a specific unique aspect of the product they're trying to sell in their sales pitches and other marketing collateral. Generally tied to differentiation, the goal is to find an aspect or element that separates your product from your competition in a manner that is so unique, it will drive a potential customer to purchase or engage.

An example: With cars, certain brands emphasize their safety protocols to exhibit their superior product. Other car brands emphasize their mileage capacity, and others still emphasize their quality. Each is communicating their unique USP.

24.

"WHITE LABEL"

White Label, or White Labeling, is when one company puts its own branding on the product manufactured by another company as if the first company was the manufacturer.

As an example, Company A produces peanut butter, and Company B has Company A produce peanut butter for it. Company A then labels the final peanut butter product under as Company B's labeling. In this instance, Company A has a White Label peanut butter product, that is, its own peanut butter brand.

White Labeling is a very common practice in many industries ranging alcohol brands to perfumes to food products. You name it, it can be White Labeled.

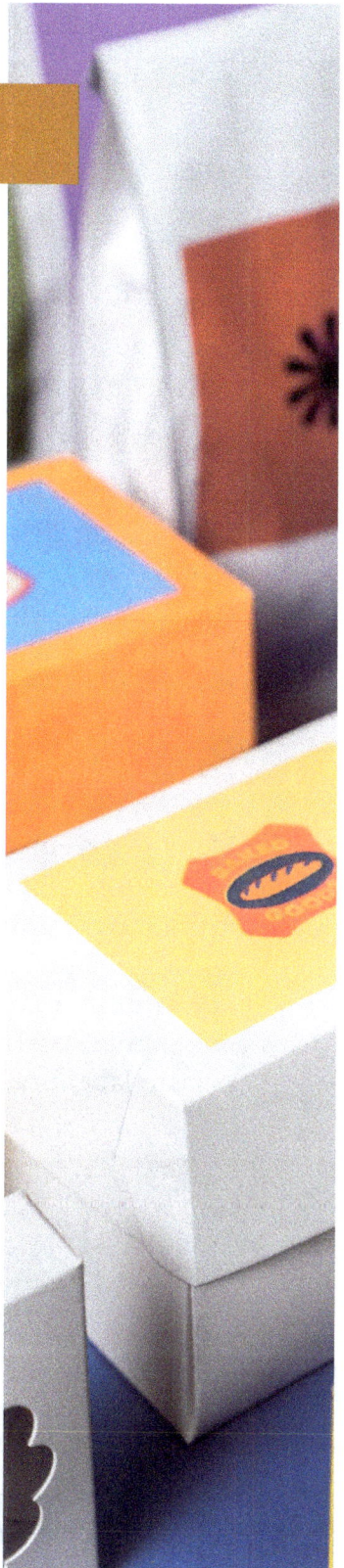

25.

"PRIVATE LABEL"

Similar to White Labeling, Private Label or Private Labeling differs from the predecessor in one very distinct way. The product that will ultimately be branded will be the exclusive formulation of the product for the branding company. Hence, the name Private Label as no other company will be able to use that specific formulation or design of a product being Private Label branded.

Many different supermarket and pharmacy chains have their own Private Label brands which represent products manufactured by another party but which are exclusively produced for the chain brand. Again this is a common practice in many industries, with many companies offering an array of products under a private label brand like Kirkland for Costco.

26.

"CONSIGNMENT"

Related to Performance-Based Compensation is Consignment, which is type of sales system where the total final amount paid for a good is related to how many of that good was sold during some agreed-to period of time.

As a common example, think of magazines, which are often sold on a Consignment agreement. The magazine vendor will carry a certain magazine on its shelves and the final price that it will pay to the publisher / producer of that magazine for a specific issue will be based on how many of that magazine were sold during the period. If it sells 10 copies it pays a price times those 10 copies only, even if it was given 30 copies to sell. This arrangement is struck to reduce the risk of vendors.

27.

"GREY MARKET"

The Grey Market, thought of as an in-between of the White Market and Black Market, is a legal market for selling goods, which differentiates it from the Black Market, but is not selling of goods through traditional approachs, which differentiates it from the White or normal market channels.

Traditionally, goods sold on the Grey Market are not authorized by the manufacturer for sale in such distribution channels, but their sales occur with some acceptance, if begrudgingly.

It is very common in certain industries like luxury goods and watches, which have authorized dealers who will unload inventory that cannot be sold to a third-party who then resells it. The resale market of these goods is the Grey Markets in this instance.

28.

"CASH COW"

Cash Cow is a phrase that describes certain products that a company sells that has been well established over time, and that generates excellent cash flow with very little Marketing investment. It is the most well-known of the quadrant names of the BCG Matrix (see next page).

Cash Cows are like business nirvana, they generate exceptional cash flow for a company but with minimal to no Marketing investment. An example could be such well-known products as Pop Tarts or Listerine or Kleenex tissues. These products are extremely well-known, they have incredible brand loyalty, and achieve great financial returns with almost no marketing. Nirvana indeed.

29.

"CAPITAL PLANNING"

Capital Planning is an essential strategy tool for businesses, large and small. As the importance of sufficient capital (cash) cannot be overstated to Businesses, wherever they are in their lifecycle, Capital Planning is the specific laying out of the projects and endeavors a business will undertake and the cash needs of each effort. The analysis will provide the total amounts needed for the company, and when they will be needed, if the analysis is completed correctly.

This is done to ensure proper funding levels for the desired projects individually, and for the company as a whole. Most company-wide strategic decisions will affected by proper Capital Planning with some projects being cancelled and others green lit.

30.

"S W.O.T. ANALYSIS"

A very insightful and thought-provoking analysis that is typically done in fuller more complete business plans, the S.W.O.T. analysis is useful both in communicating to outside investors, but also to inside management.

(S)trengths.
(W)eaknesses.
(O)pportunities.
(T)hreats.

By first analyzing, then by attempting to communicate each of these four areas to investors, Management gives a very precise picture of the landscape a business must compete on. Additionally the S.W.O.T Analysis acts as an on-going guide and reference material to strategy.

31.

"MINIMUM VIABLE PRODUCT (MVP)"

In the Sports world, MVP stands for Most Valuable Player. In a business, MVP is Minimum Viable Product.

The Minimum Viable Product represents the most basic version of a product. It has useful necessary features to create interest. In essence, the product is sufficient to show investors, but it is by definition not the best the product will be in the future, and probably not ready for the market.

Oftentimes companies will launch with their MVP in order to be the first mover in a new product category, so thereby building an early following and capturing early adopters. But most times companies launch the MVP to start generating cash flow from a product or project that is utilizing limited resources such as cash or time.

32.

"MINIMUM MARKETABLE PRODUCT (MMP)"

The next stage in the evolution of a company's new product is when undeniably the company has a product that can go to market, when it is at the stage of Minimum Marketable Product (MMP). This is when a company feels the product has enough development, enough interesting features and quality so that interested target audiences will be willing to pay money for the product.

Clearly the MMP is a stage after the Minimum Viable Product for most products. It is the point where the company should begin to make Marketing investments to actively market the product to its target audience.

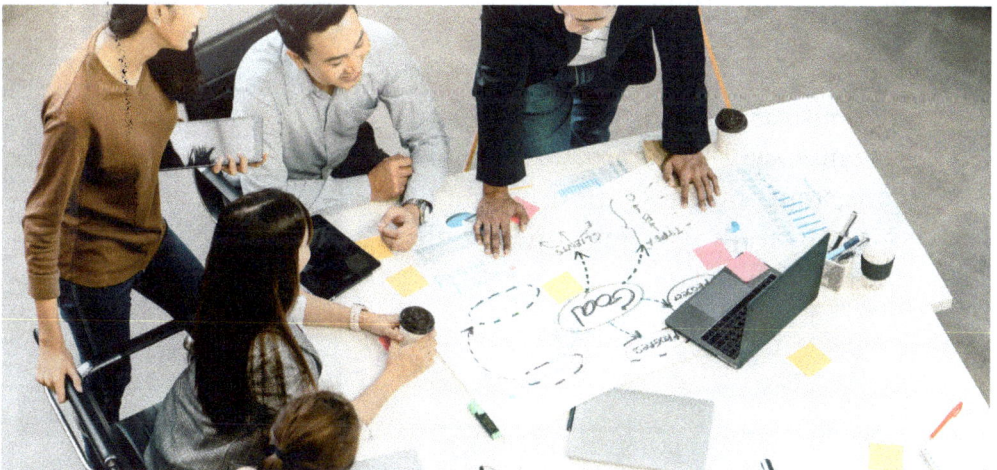

33.

"SPECIALIZATION"

An old business adage says that diversification is the only free lunch. But Specialization is the key to a successful business launch, and is a strategy approach for all Small Businesses to consider firmly.

Specialization is limiting either the business model or the product offerings to a specific area of expertise or market interest. This limitation focuses all efforts and investments on fewer activities, which tends to drive better results in the short term, be it marketing or cash utilization.

It is true that over time diversification of assets and revenue, will generate safer, more consistent business returns. But Specialization is where one should start.

30

34.

"PROOF OF CONCEPT (POC)"

In any new business model, and also every new business as well, there is a level of belief needed that shows the idea or business is viable. By viable, there are different levels, but Proof of Concept is one level where viability has been demonstrated. In Business, it is not until POC is achieved that some Investors will even consider a new venture for potential investment.

For new products, Proof of Concept can mean that the product is technologically proven, or perhaps a prototype works sufficiently well. For new Businesses, POC can mean the business has proven that it can generate some level of financial progress, be it sales, gross margin or profitability.

35.

"THE RECURRING REVENUE MODEL"

Perhaps the most beloved business model these days by investors is known as the Recurring Revenue model and its popularity can be seen in the change in models all around the business world. It is in essence a subscription model, be it monthly or annual, where customers pay on a recurring basis for a product or service as opposed to a one-time purchase of the product or service.

The Recurring Revenue model is seen everywhere now, in software subscriptions and electronic products which had previously been priced through paying once and done strategy.

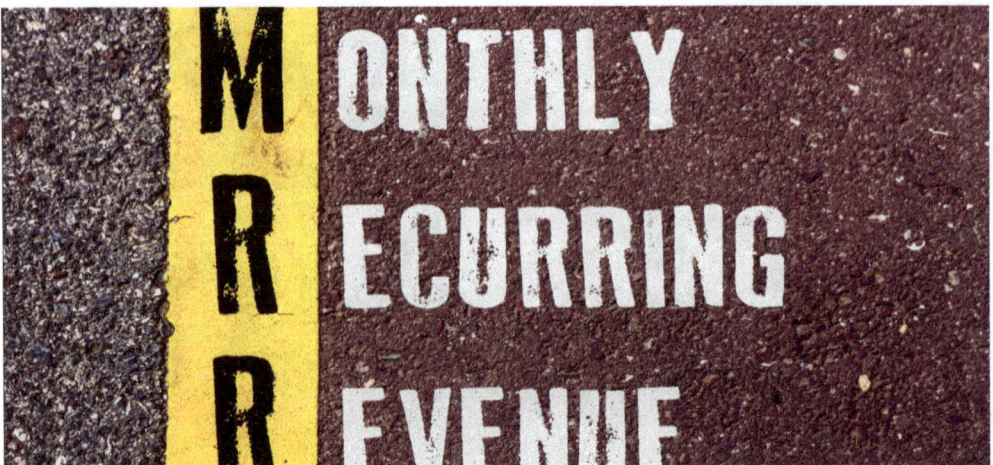

MANAGEMENT

BUSINESS BASICS EXPLAINED SIMPLY

1.

"THE 80-20 RULE"

In general, the idea here is that 80% of some output will come from 20% of some input. Essentially it is a rule of thumb that the majority of something comes from a minority of something.

In business we tend to believe that 80% of your sales comes from 20% of your customers. Hence The 80-20 Rule. This is often true for Small Businesses, where one large company can dominate the Total Sales of the company.

The corresponding lesson is that one must really take care of those 20% of your customers who are giving your business 80% of its sales revenue.

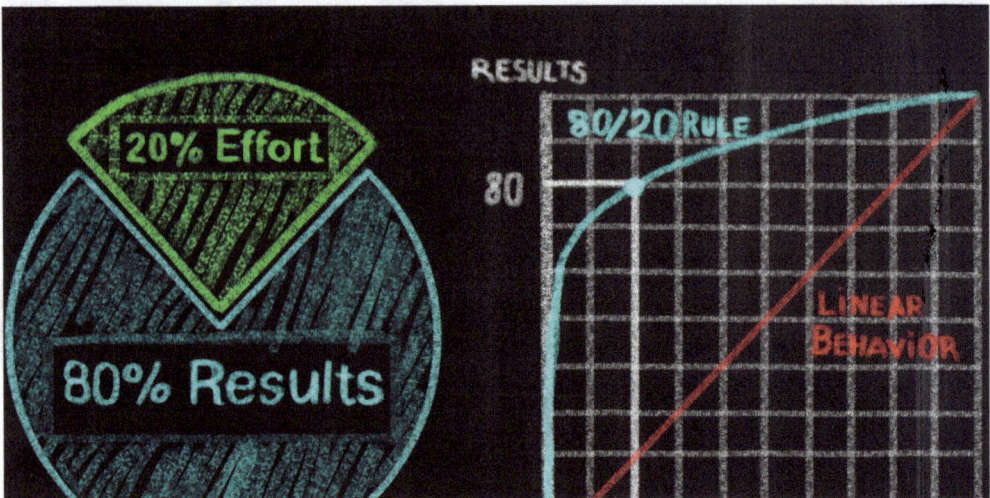

2.

"CUSTOMER RESOURCE MANAGEMENT SYSTEM (CRM)"

Customer Resource Management systems, known by the acronym CRM, is a software program that aids a company in dealing with its customer base by acting as a repository of all the important information for all of its clients.

Though they come in different shapes and sizes, most CRMs are very useful for Small Businesses to track important information about their clients including contact information, the last communication and past order history. When used effectively, CRMs help a company manage the relationship with its customers leading to better loyalty and sales.

There are free CRMs available on the Internet for download.

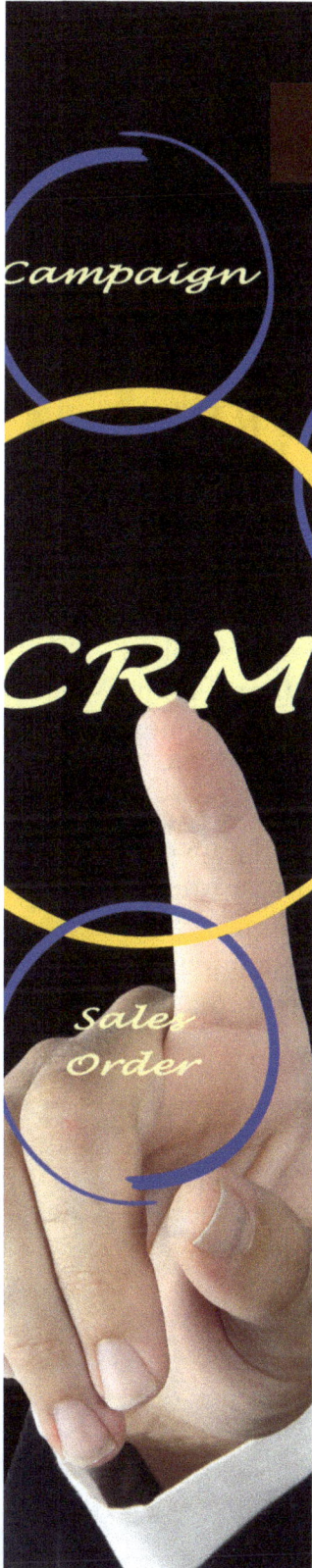

3.

"BARRIERS TO ENTRY"

Barriers to Entry is a competition strategy term that defines a group of elements that a company or project has that impede the entry into the market of competitors or a competitive product. Investors prefer to invest in companies that have excellent Barriers to Entry though in reality, there is no complete barrier to entry. With enough money, every barrier can be overcome.

Some of the most effective Barriers to Entry include First Mover status, large capital investments, governmental hurdles and enforceable patents. Each of these acts a hindrance to a some competitor entering the marketing without forbidding it totally.

4.

"FIRST MOVER STATUS"

First Mover Status is a major competitor defense, often called a Barrier to Entry, as it acts as a barrier against competitors entering a marketplace.

In essence, a company launches its product first into a marketplace or segment within a marketplace thereby giving the company a chance to promote its product while the customers have no other option besides the company's product. Think Tesla.

By moving first, a company can garner all of the attention, and all of the sales, and the hope is the first movement will give the company such a lead that competitors will hesitate and even decide not to enter the marketplace because the first mover has so established itself in the target market's mind.

5.

"NON-DISCLOSURE & CONFIDENTIALITY AGREEMENTS"

NDA stands for Non-Disclosure Agreement, and along with Confidentiality Agreements, which are similar and often serve the same purpose, aim to protect the proprietary ideas behind a company and its product offerings. It is recommended strongly that all businesses use them.

Protected information such as trade secrets, marketing plans, computer programming can be extremely valuable to the company developing them. NDAs and CAs are stand-alone documents, or just even added language in other agreements, that work to set-up a barrier to counterparties to an agreement using or sharing protected information without approval.

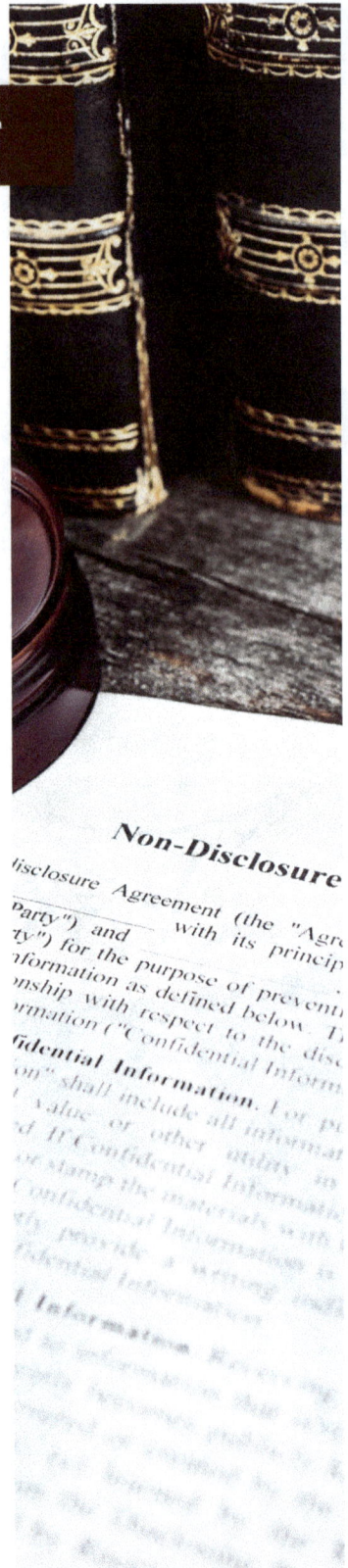

6.

"DIVERSIFICATION"

Most often thought of in a Financial Investment context, Diversification has much broader and important aspects for a business as a whole. Simply, Diversification means the spreading out of some element across different sources. Management diversifies generally in business to reduce risks.

Some examples: It is very important to diversify revenue streams among different products, and production capacities over different suppliers. Even diversifying into different business lines, and yes, investment categories, allows businesses to protect themselves against a host of issues that arise from too much consolidation in one source.

7.

"DUE DILIGENCE"

An essential step in so many aspects of running a business, choosing partners and suppliers, and making investments, Due Diligence is the act of investigating a counterparty and their claims about themselves.

We run our businesses under the banner of Trust but verify, and the verification process is Due Diligence. It can be myriad activities, but often it includes reviewing their bank statements, existing contracts, and tax returns. Also often we talk with partners, outside investors, even suppliers external to the company.

Every sales pitch has some fluff, even yours and mine. Due Diligence limits the risks and secures your efforts. Do it. Do it thoroughly. You'll regret it if you don't.

8.

"LEARNING CURVES"

Most broadly defined as the understanding that we humans get better at things the more we do them. The more we study welding, the better we get at welding. We talk of "riding the Learning Curve," benefiting from experience.

In Business, we talk of steep or shallow Learning Curves, which represent the proportion of the speed and incline of the curve. Learn fast, improve a lot quickly, and the benefits are exponential. Learn more slowly, improve incrementally, and you may be out of business before you get to where you need to be to succeed.

Ride the Learning Curve as fast as you can and reap the rewards.

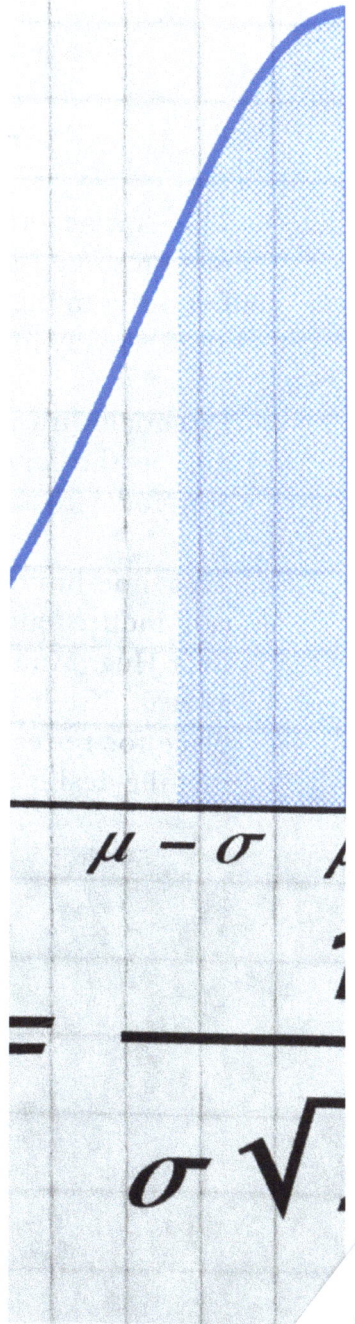

223

9.

"BEAR HUG"

This is a negotiating tactic, and sadly, a very effective one on some inexperienced negotiators. It's used most famously in big Wall Street acquisitions, but works just as effectively in Small Business environments.

Essentially it's pressure applied to a counterparty to a deal in the form of, "Here's our offer. You have until 5pm today to accept it or it expires forever."

This time-limited pressure, a form of 'take it or leave it' can induce enormous pressure, hence the phrase, a Bear Hug. And it is effective, if the threat is perceived as real. Use it yourselves, but judiciously. It leaves no place for retreat. If the deadline is passed, your word that the deal is dead must be true.

10.

"OPERATING LEVERAGE"

Operating Leverage is a measurement of how a company is affected by an increase in sales and/or margin. If the company's success is highly affected by a change in revenue, it is said to have high Operating Leverage. Conversely, if the opposite occurs, a company is not positively affected by a substantial change in revenue it is said to have low Operating Leverage. Often the effect is driven by debt amounts.

Largely, this is a function of the overall gross margin the company's able to achieve on the products it sells. If a company is able to adjust its sales through the increase in sales' high margin products as opposed to low margin products, it is increasing its Operating Leverage. It's essentially becoming more efficient of turning sales into gross margin.

11.

"E.S.G."

The acronym ESG stands for Environmental, Societal, and Corporate Governence, and together it is a school of thought speaking to and asking for responsible business activities in various areas of business procedures and investing. The areas often are concerned with issues such as global warming, drug and sex trafficking, child labor and underaged employment issues and other social societal concerns.

Many companies now, especially investment companies, are developing strategies to ensure their business practices and even investment choices, either reflect or are outright designed to ensure adherence to practices and policies that take what is believed to be a positive stance in societal matters.

12.

"BUSINESS CREDIBILITY"

An incalculably important element for success, Business Credibility, is defined as the trust and believability manifested in a target audience for a company or its products. Specifically, it is the belief that a company can fulfill the claims and promises made in its marketing campaigns.

Achieving Business Credibility is a function of the classic phrase, "Doing what you say you're going to do, as you said you would do it." All consumers, in all fields, make purchasing decisions based on the belief that a product or a company will deliver on what it has promised. When companies break this covenant, there is mistrust and disbelief which are deadly aspects for businesses, as Business Credibility is incredibly difficult to recover once lost.

13.

"PERISHABILITY"

In Business, the concept of Perishability relates specifically to the nature of certain inventory that companies keep that lose their value over time. While it is often more easy to understand in terms of inventory, like fruits and vegetables, one must remember that other inventory items in different industries such as fashion and entertainment feel the effects of Perishability.

In those industries when Perishability is a factor, good managers are tracking their inventory in light of and with an eye towards the timeline of the inventory, where it is in its "saleable" life. So often thereafter strategic decisions are made with respect to marketing, often pricing in particular, to move the deteriorating inventory so a total loss does not occur.

14.

"PURPOSE-DRIVEN BUSINESS"

While not necessarily a not-for-profit company, a Purpose-Driven business is a business equally or even more interested in doing some defined objective (purpose) greater than profits. Often they are non-for-profit companies, but it is possible to be Purpose-Driven and still generate profits.

Oftentimes, the Purpose-Driven business is focused on helping society as a whole. Modern examples are climate change driven companies, and literary and learning based companies.

Many think that a purpose that drives and animates corporate policy is an essential element for success in the current corporate culture.

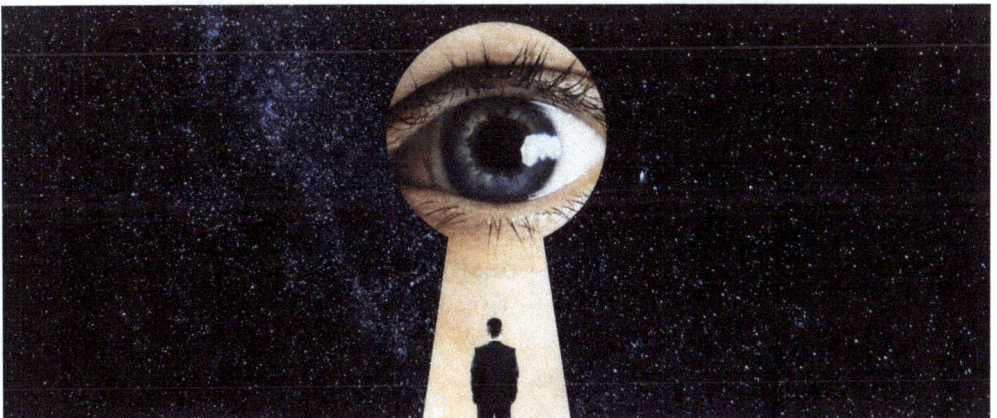

15.

"LIMITED LIABILITY COMPANY (LLC)"

The legal structure most popular with small business owners is Limited Liability Companies, known as LLCs, because it allows the business owner increased protection from liabilities while also treating them similar to a sole proprietor on a tax basis. The key benefits to this legal structure are protections and tax treatment.

Hence the name, Limited Liability companies limit the liability the company owner faces to only the assets of the company, and not the personal assets of the owner. Additionally the income (or loss) of these companies are passed through to the owners individually, so the company does not pay taxes per se, but the owner(s) themselves are responsible, which can have tax benefits.

16.

"NOT-FOR-PROFIT COMPANY"

A Not-For-Profit company is a legal structure for companies where the company states in its filings that it has been granted a beneficial tax structure as a result of it not producing profits. Known in America as a 501c3 company, the company agrees to forgo excessive profit generation in lieu of this favorable tax structure.

Most charitable companies use this corporate structure for their activities as it provides them protection from certain liabilities while retaining the beneficial tax status. It's important to note that Not-For-Profit companies can lose their Not-For-Profit beneficial tax status if the activities and limitations on profit are not adhered to.

17.

"S CORPORATION"

Often thought of as a hybrid between an LLC and a C corporation, an S Corporation shares some qualities of both of the other structures. For tax purposes, S Corporations are pass-through companies so the entity is not taxed, but the shareholders who own the company are taxed on their personal tax filings. Of course, liability limitation/protection is similar to other corporate structures.

Additionslly, S Corporations are limited in the number of shareholders they can have to the total of 100 whereas C Corporations are unlimited. Shareholders in S Corporations must be actual human individuals, meaning they cannot be another legal entity such as an LLC, a C Corporation or another S Corporation. C Corps do not have this restriction.

18.

"C CORPORATION"

Generally, the company structure for the largest companies in the world, C Corporations are the most formal and the most difficult to maintain corporate structure, as financial and tax reporting requirements tend to be the most strict. Unlike other legal structures, C Corporations file taxes themselves as opposed to passing through to owners in the other legal structures (LLCs, S Corporations).

C Corporations can have unlimited shareholders in the company as opposed to S Corporations, which are limited to just 100. C Corporations can have other legal entities as shareholders, for example, other C Corps. Further, C Corps can have multiple classes of stocks. None of the other legal structures are allowed these various options.

19.

"SKU'S"

The acronym stands for Stock Keeping Units. SKUs are numbers that represent specific product variations. It can be different products, but more detailed and granular, it is often different versions of the same product.

Example: If a company sells four different shirts, and sells each of those four in five different colors, the resulting number of different products on offer, thereby SKUs, is 20.

Each variation is a SKU because the company will need to keep inventory of each different shirt in each different color. A system of SKUs is essential for tracking sales, ordering new inventory, and even accounting correctly for product effects on the company.

20.

"PERFORMANCE-BASED COMPENSATION"

Performance-Based Compensation is when a supplier of some good or service is paid based on achieving certain results. Most commonly, it is related to payments made to employees or consultants. When based on sales made, that is called commissions.

However, it is also possible that the supplying and paying for actual physical profits can be Performance-Based. In these instances companies can pay for products solely based on how many they sell of that product. With Performance-Based Compensation it is important to note that if the metric agreed upon is not achieved, no payment can be made.

21.

"COMPARATIVE ADVANTAGE"

The economic concept of Comparative Advantage is a key management principle. While it generally applies to countries and trade, the principal has benefits for business managing. In essence, it is the principal that a manager or a business should do what it does best and in the greatest proportion relative to a different party.

For example, one company produces one necessary product substantially better (more effective, cheaper) than another company, but doesn't produce a different necessary product equally better. The first company should focus on producing the first product and let the other company produce the second product. It is the same with employees.

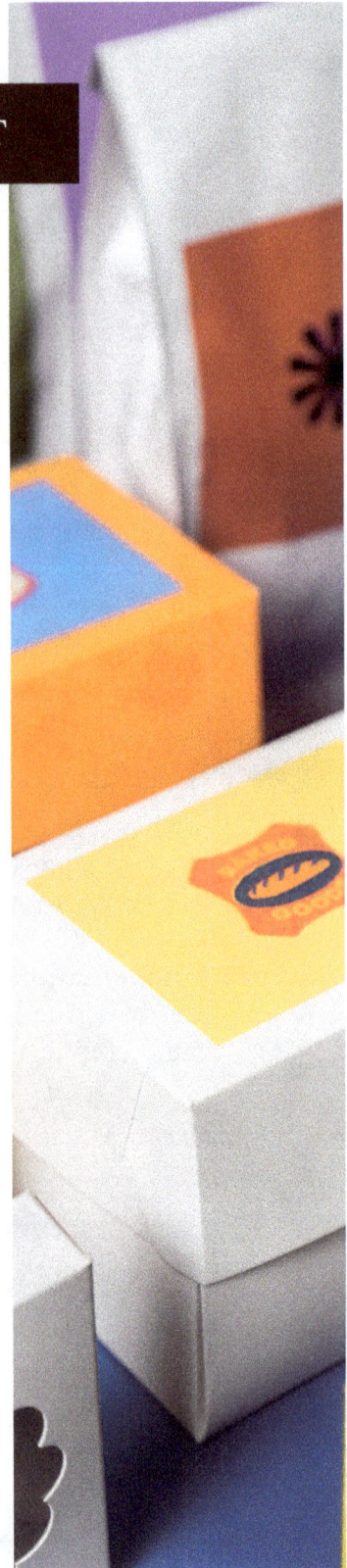

22.

"BANKRUPTCY"

When businesses can no longer make payments on their debt, and they have no access to other cash to fund their business, they will have to declare Bankruptcy. In the United States there are different forms of Bankruptcy, one that deals with the liquidation of the company and its assets, and one that allows the company to reduce or "reorganize" its debts, but continue its operations known as a reorganization.

It is important to note that the Bankruptcy of a company does not affect the personal asset holdings of the shareholders. It is merely the assets and operations of the company itself that are affected unless illegal conduct has occurred. Personal Bankruptcy is different than its corporate versions.

23.

"EVERGREEN"

Evergreen is the business concept pertaining to certain assets and projects that generate a good consistent return on investment over a long period of time without much effort or input needed to continue the return. These assets are very highly-prized by investors, though often are difficult to purchase or create.

Take for example a patent for a unique product where the design can be licensed out to users who wish to pay a royalty to use the design. The owner of this patent essentially does nothing, makes no effort or investment, yet receives payments from the users. It is an Evergreen generating consistent cash flow with minimal effort.

As Business people, we love this.

24.

"LETTER OF INTENT (L.O.I)"

In business, a Letter of Intent is a document signed between two parties (companies or individuals), to express their intention for an asset or equity sale. When one company is looking to work with or purchase some or all of the shares of another company, they will often sign a Letter of Intent to express their full interest in purchasing part of the company to the company and to a third party like a bank. It will have the terms of the potential deal.

It is important to note that the LOI is a non-binding agreement which means it only expresses intent to do something and is not an obligation to do something.

25.

"GOVERNING LAW"

An important element of every business contract, Governing Law states laws will be paramount in case of a dispute between businesses in different states. Many aspects of business law vary from state to state with each state having different rules, regulations, and elements of law.

Even further, many times different states have laws that are in conflict with each other. So it is important to expressly state in the contract which state is the governor law.

When a contract explicitly states which state law governs, if a dispute arises, the laws of the specific state will be that which the court will interpret the contract, and will mandate where the court case and trial will be adjudicated.

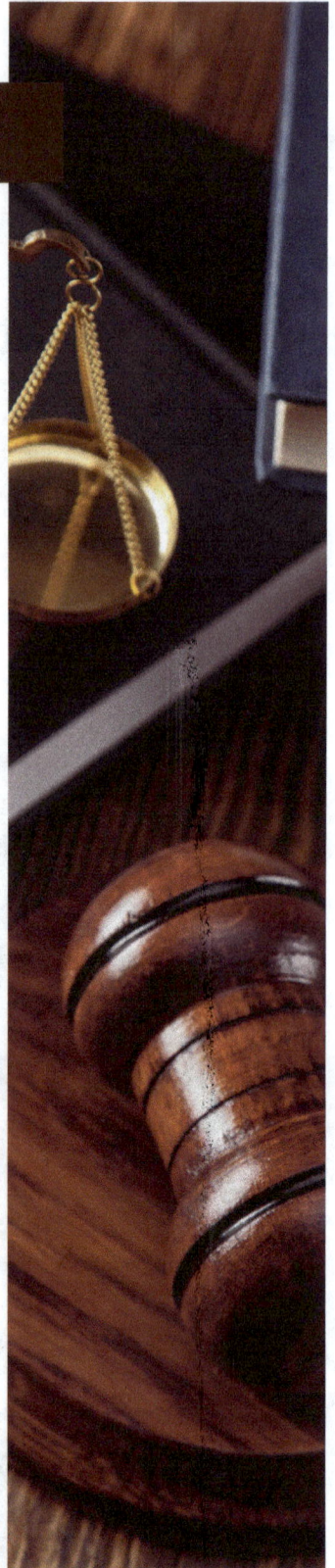

26.

"INDEMNIFICATION"

As an extremely important clause in most well-written contracts, Indemnification (from the verb, to indemnify), protects one party of the contract from the behaviors and actions of the other party of the contract. When signed, it is a legally binding element of protection.

By signing a single or mutual Indemnification clause, one party to the contract must indemnify, make whole, pay the fees, fines and judgements for the other party of the contract if the first party's actions caused harm for which both parties are held liable and legally responsible.

With risky counter parties to contracts, an Indemnification clause can be a company saver.

27.

"R.O.T.I"

Everyone remembers to focus on R.O.I., Return on Investment, and rightly so. But far too many forget about R.O.T.I., Return on Time Investment, and for Small Businesses, it is equally essential. It compares the financial return on an investment with the amount of time it takes to achieve that return.

Time is as limited and as limiting as cash in a Small Business and Small Businesspeople must make decisions constantly about whether a project, a client, or an investment is not only worth it on a financial perspective, but also on a time perspective. Will the R.O.T.I. be sufficient?

There is a Time Opportunity cost of pursuing things that are not worth the effort, so calculate R.O.T.I to ensure proper time investments.

28.

"SUPPLY, DEMAND, SCARCITY, ABUNDANCE"

These powerful economic concepts have real life consequences and implications for small businesses in all areas of a business, from sales and marketing to inventory management to Capital allocations. All goods and services that exist in a marketplace are affected by Supply (the amount of these available), Demand (the amount desired), and relative Scarcity and Abundance (imbalances between the other two, the first deficiency and the second, excess).

In times of abundance or scarcity as a result of supply and demand imbalances, business managers will need to adjust strategies to account for that business landscape and its potential effect on their business.

BALANCE

SUPPLY

DEMAND

29.

"MILESTONE TRACKING"

Milestone Tracking is an excellent tool that business managers can use to measure progress towards stated goals of the company. Additionally, it is something investors are very interested in reviewing before investing.

In essence, Milestone Tracking is the process of developing and writing down milestones, those events that evince a level of progress for a company. To be done well, a milestone must have specific, particular levels in some area of the business. An example could be achieving the first $20,000 in sales. Another could be finishing a prototype of a new product for launch. The key is in the importance of the event and the specificity in the target.

30.

"COST-BENEFIT ANALYSIS (CBA)"

An essential Business Analysis, with offshoots in real life too, Cost-Benefit Analysis is an analyzation of a decision weighing all its costs against the benefits that come from the decision. Of course, one should look for decisions that generate not only a positive benefit total but even greater than just a little positive.

Be it construction projects, hiring employees, doing marketing campaigns and countless other vital business decisions, understanding and comparing the costs to be invested against the benefits that can be expected from the investment made is a core Management task that must be learned, implemented and followed.

31.

"RISK MANAGEMENT"

Risk Management is one of the preemptive responsibilities of senior management in a company. Some would say that Risk Management, managing the amount of risk in given situations and the company as a whole, is the key role of a board of directors.

Companies manage risk time managing their cash flow, deciding which strategic projects to take on and which to pass and ensuring that proper management is in place to avoid improper decisions and actions. Such things as compliance departments and insurance policies are some of the tools companies use to manage risk. A strong combination of Corporate oversight and strategic analysis are essential elements to ensure a company can achieve it's objectives in ethical and profitable manners.

32.

"DECKCHAIRING"

Related to the musicians on the Titanic who remained playing music while the steamship sank, Deckchairing is a new term, a neologism, in the business lexicon (sorry, some big words there). But it is an essential concept or fault to look out for, and adjust when it arrives.

Deckchairing is when someone can't stop making minor changes to some project, essentially working on that project too long, while achieving nothing of any major value with the continued efforts. It's important to recognize when we're doing this, because time is a substantial limitation for all small business people. So if your efforts are making little to no difference, stop, move on to the next step or phase or something that may make meaningful value to your business.

33.

"N-OF-1 THINKING"

In the field of Statistics, the letter N stands for sample size, the number of respondents or observations in the survey. Normally one wants a very large N to ensure sufficient diversity in a study. The opposite of a very large N is N=1.

N=1, or N-of-1 Thinking is when a person believes that their sole experience speaks for the larger population. This is a fallacy that many new and Small Business people make and it is something to fight against. "I like this so everyone will like this." Ensure that experiences or thoughts are sufficiently shared by a large enough sample size to increase the chances of success for a project or business venture.

34.

"LEASE (RENT) VS. BUY ANALYSIS"

Another essential Business analysis, Lease vs. Buy Analysis compares capital allocation strategies for Small Businesses as pertains to capital investments. With many essential capital investments a business must make, a company has a choice between leasing a product or buying it outright.

Examples are plentiful. Cars, Capital equipment like large copiers and printing equipment, and even office space which can be rented or purchased, Businesses can and should complete Lease vs. Buy analyses which calculate the costs and the benefits of each strategy with respect to capital investment. Considerations such as capital availability and long-term growth expectations affect these decisions.

35.

"FORCE MAJEURE"

Force Majeure is a legal concept that finds itself in many contracts between supplying companies and their purchasing clients, and it pertains to default provisions if one company cannot deliver as a contract delineates that they should. Essentially, Force Majeure frees a company from liability if some extraordinary event occurs that prohibits one party to a contract from delivering as prescribed in an agreement due to unforeseen circumstances.

An example: A company has ordered a container ship of new cars, but there is a typhoon at sea and the container ship is sunk. The delivering party will declare a Force Majeure event, which frees the delivering party from liability of non-delivery. In essence, extreme events beyond the normal control of one party (national strike, war, weather extremity).

36.

"JOINT VENTURE (JV)"

When two separate, distinct companies come together to invest in a third company, this third company is a Joint Venture. Generally but not always, the shares in the JV, as it's often referred to, are equally distributed between the two investing companies.

There are many various reasons why companies will do Joint Ventures together. Some of the most common are the sharing of costs and expenses on a project that will take substantial investments. Other times it's because the partner companies have different technologies that can partner well so the JV shares the disparate technologies.

Always the JV will have an operating agreement which explains such matters as roles, investments, and ownership stake and Buy-out Mechanisms.

37.

"BUY-OUT MECHANISM"

In most companies' shareholder or operating agreements, certainly those that are partnerships, there is often what is known as a Buy-out Mechanism clause. This is a defined calculation whereby one or more shareholders can Buy-out the shares of another or multiple other shareholders.

This specific detailed Buy-out Mechanism is agreed to by all parties in advance, and is memorialized clearly in the company's agreements.

The mechanism calculations can vary greatly in structure and substance. An example would be some multiple (let's say 12x) times next year's projected EBITDA.

38.

"RISK ADVERSE / RISK TOLERANT"

Opposite sides of the Risk spectrum coin, Risk Averse and Risk Tolerant describe the attitude of someone to risk and the chances of a risky event occurring in business / investments.

Risk Adverse describes someone who is not interested and against taking on projects, investments, etc. that contain a greater than average risk profile. This means when risks are great, there is a greater than average chance of failure or loss of money.

People who are Risk Tolerant are open to taking on projects, investments, etc. that are riskier than average, where the chance of failure and loss of money is not insubstantial and may be greater than average.

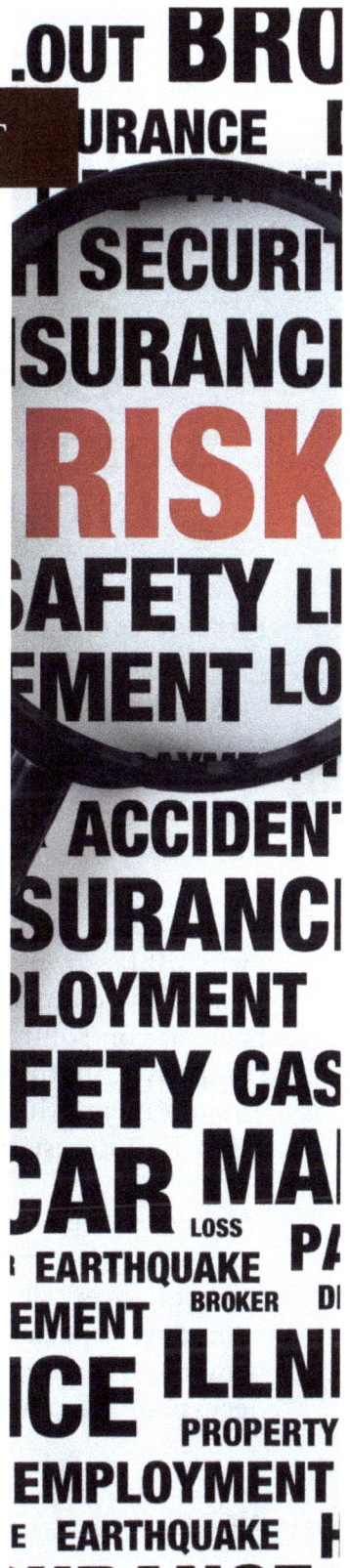

39.

"CONTROLLING INTEREST"

As with all things, we can only have 100% of something, and so is true with businesses. Thus there can only be a 100% ownership percentage of a company, no matter how many shareholders there are. The total outstanding percentages will equal 100%.

When some person or company owns 50.1% or more of the voting shares in a company, it is said they have a controlling interest in the company. Anything less than this amount means the shareholder has a Minority Interest, even if it's 49.9%.

Having a Controlling Interest, allows that entity, person or company "control" over all decisions in the company, especially those over the company's strategic direction that necessitate shareholder votes.

40.

"MINORITY STAKE / MINORITY INTEREST"

In contrast to a Controlling Interest, which is owning more than 50%, a Minority Interest is when a person or company owns less than 50% of the outstanding voting shares of a company. This leaves the majority of the shares with other owners.

This Minority Stake has certain legal rights, but since it does not have more than 50% of the voting shares, it can leave a shareholder in a precarious state as the majority shareholder or shareholder group can ultimately decide what happens on matters related to the company. However, it's very common that a person or company with a Minority Interest can partner with other shareholders with whom they develop, in effect, a controlling interest group.

41.

"SUBSIDIARY COMPANIES / SUBSIDIARY LLCS"

Subsidiary Companies are companies where the shares in the company are owned by another company in whole or in majority part. The company that owns the shares, usually called the Parent company, controls what happens in the subsidiary. This can give it control over its investments, operations and profits. Often Subsidiary Companies are setup through this legal structure to limit the liability of the parent companies that own them.

A Subsidiary LLC is where an LLC is owned by another LLC. The rules that govern LLCs are state specific, and the rules will apply to the subsidiary LLC as it does to the patent LLC.

42.

"BENCHMARKING"

One of the most effective live tools of corporate management is to set Benchmarks and track progress against the chosen Benchmarks. This analytical act of comparing your company's result to the Benchmarks setup is known as Benchmarking.

Oftentimes they will set up their own benchmarks for comparison, and other times they will look for their specific industry's standards or their direct competitive figures for comparison.

Examples can include obvious metrics like profitability and revenue, but softer targets like Social Media followers or email addresses for a mail list are also important end effective figures to Benchmark against.

43.

"MALFEASANCE, FRAUD, MALPRACTICE"

An essential understanding of what constitutes Fraud, Malfeasance and Malpractice, all various types of negligence, is vital to have in the field of business management. For as much as we would like it to not be the case, far too often these words come into play in business activities. They represent unfair and illegal practices taken by one party to an agreement or understanding against another.

Malfeasance is when you act improperly in a position in which you have been appointed, (for example, stealing). Malpractice is when you have acted improperly against someone in the professional service you offer. Fraud is the deliberate cheating or misleading of another party to an arrangement or agreement.

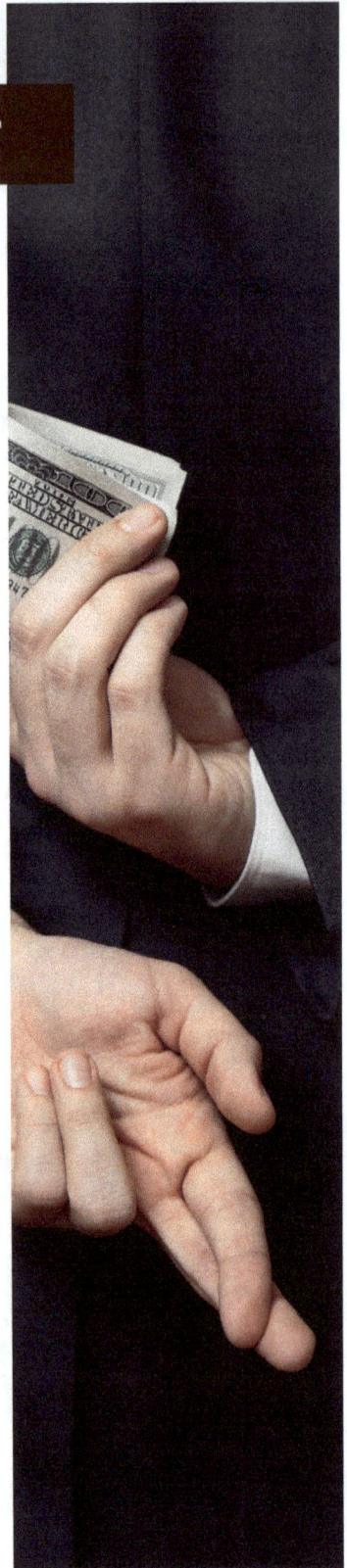

ABOUT THE AUTHOR

Mr. Goldstein is currently the President and Founder of Goldart Consulting LLC, a Small Business consulting firm specializing in marketing, finance, strategy & management consulting to micro and small businesses start-up operation. Current and past clients are based throughout America, as well as in many countries in Europe and Asia. He has helped Small Businesses generate many millions in revenue and profits.

Previously, as the Director of Financial Planning and Analysis at SFX Entertainment Inc., a forerunner to Live Nation Inc., Mr. Goldstein helped analyze and complete over $3 billion in Merger and Acquisition activity including the acquisition of the industry's leading concert promoters and entertainment companies such as Bill Graham Presents, PACE Entertainment, Contemporary Productions, Don Law, & David Falk Mgmt.

Prior to this, Mr. Goldstein was the Manager of Strategic Planning in Corporate Sales and Marketing at Cablevision Systems, then the country's fifth largest cable system and owner of several Entertainment assets including the Madison Square Garden, Radio City Music Hall, the New York Knicks and Rangers, and the American Movie Classics and Bravo television channels.

Mr. Goldstein has a Masters of Business Administration in Finance from New York University and a Bachelor of Science in Management in Marketing from Tulane University in New Orleans.

ALSO FROM GOLDART PUBLISHING

SMALL BUSINESS SUCCESS SERIES

250 BUSINESS BASICS EXPLAINED SIMPLY
KEY WORDS, CONCEPTS & IDEAS TO UNLOCK YOUR LITERACY, KNOWLEDGE AND CAPACITY IN THE CHANGING SMALL BUSINESS WORLD
SMALL BUSINESS SUCCESS SERIES: PART I
STUART GOLDSTEIN, MBA
CEO, GOLDART CONSULTING LLC
SMALL BUSINESS SPECIALISTS

201 SMALL BUSINESS TIPS TO LIVE BY
BATTLE-TESTED ADVICE TO HELP SMALL BUSINESSES, START-UPS, & ENTREPRENEURS SURVIVE AND THRIVE
SMALL BUSINESS SUCCESS SERIES: PART II
STUART GOLDSTEIN, MBA
CEO, GOLDART CONSULTING LLC
SMALL BUSINESS SPECIALISTS

100 ESSENTIAL TIPS FOR A BETTER BUSINESS PLAN
BATTLE-TESTED ADVICE FOR BETTER BUSINESS PLANS THAT WILL ACHIEVE GOALS FROM PLANNING TO FUND RAISING
SMALL BUSINESS SUCCESS SERIES: PART III
STUART GOLDSTEIN
CEO, GOLDART CONSULTING LLC
SMALL BUSINESS SPECIALISTS

1 PERSON BUSINESSES 200 ESSENTIALS
THE KEY WORDS, CORE GUIDANCE AND HELPFUL TIPS FOR BEGINNERS TO SURVIVE AND THRIVE AS SOLO ENTREPRENEURS
STUART GOLDSTEIN, MBA
CEO, GOLDART CONSULTING LLC
SMALL BUSINESS SPECIALISTS

INVESTING FOR BEGINNERS SERIES

250 INVESTING: ESSENTIAL BASICS
THE KEY DEFINITIONS, CONCEPTS, IDEAS, AND FOUNDATIONS FOR NEW INVESTOR SUCCESS
INVESTING FOR BEGINNERS SERIES: PART I
STUART GOLDSTEIN, MBA
CEO, GOLDART CONSULTING LLC
SMALL BUSINESS SPECIALISTS

101 INVESTING TIPS TO LIVE BY
KEY AXIOMS, INSIGHTS, AND FUNDAMENTAL COUNSEL FOR NEW INVESTOR SUCCESS
INVESTING FOR BEGINNERS SERIES: PART II
STUART GOLDSTEIN, MBA
CEO, GOLDART CONSULTING LLC
SMALL BUSINESS SPECIALISTS

INVESTING COMPLETE THE COMBINED EDITION
THE KEY DEFINITIONS, CONCEPTS, IDEAS GUIDANCE & COUNSEL FOR NEW INVESTOR SUCCESS
STUART GOLDSTEIN, MBA
CEO, GOLDART CONSULTING LLC
SMALL BUSINESS SPECIALISTS

All books available on Amazon in Kindle ebook, and both Black & White and vibrant Full Color Paperback editions. Some titles are available on our website in lower-priced downloadable PDF version.

www.goldartpub.com

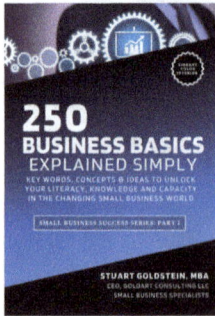

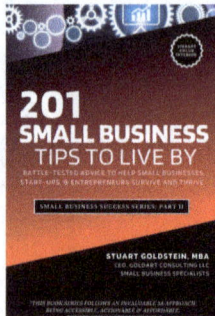

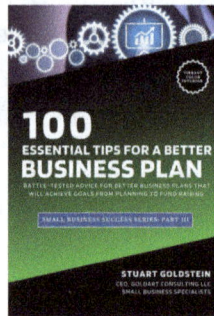

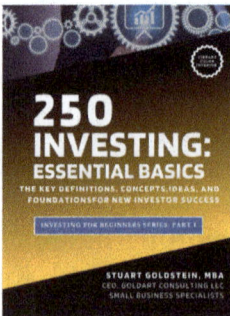

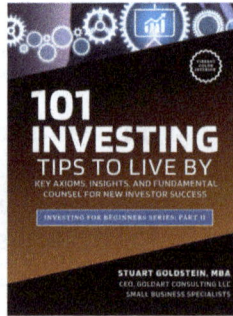

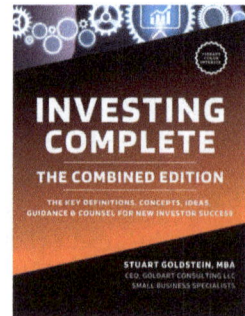

THANK YOUS & ACKNOWLEDGEMENTS

I would like to thank enormously the following, which helped make this endeavor possible and cost effective:

CANVA SOFTWARE: This is an incredible software program and application that allows one to build graphic projects such as this book. The paid-tier is even better as it allows you a ton of free photos for use.

PIXABAY: This is a magnificent site allows you to download free photos for use in products such as this.

Thank you to my many clients over the years, who have been the sounding board and on the receiving end of these "Tips" as I created and refined them.

ABOUT THE PUBLISHER: GOLDART PUBLISHING LLC

Goldart Publishing LLC is a sister company of Goldart Consulting LLC, a Small Business Consulting practice specializing in Finance, Marketing, Strategic Planning and Management. It was started 22 years ago with the goal of bringing the latest in Enterprise advisory, the skills, practices and efforts, oftentimes the difference between success and failure, to Small Businesses companies at a cost that is not prohibitive. Over these years, we have helped countless Enterprises in myriad industries and countries accomplish the goals they've set out to achieve.

Please feel free to contact us if you need
help with your Small or Mid-sized Business
Goldart Consulting LLC
(888) 203 -6419
www.goldartcconsulting.com

www.ingramcontent.com/pod-product-compliance
Lightning Source LLC
Chambersburg PA
CBHW061207220326
41597CB00015BA/1544